Fun Math problems for 5 - 8 grades.

Just solve problems!
Beat your classmates!
Be admitted to top schools!

Inna Shapiro

Fun Math problems for 5-8 grades.

Copyright © 2008 by Inna Shapiro

All rights reserved.

No part of this book may be reproduced in any form or by any electronic or mechanical means including information storage and retrieval systems, without permission in writing from the author.

Requests for permission to translate into another language or to make copies of any part of this book should be mailed to shapinna@gmail.com

ISBN 978-0-6152-1773-4

Contents

Part 1   Logical problems   5

Part 2   Cutting   25

Part 3   Drawing   45

Part 4   Chessboard problems   66

Part 5   Pouring   90

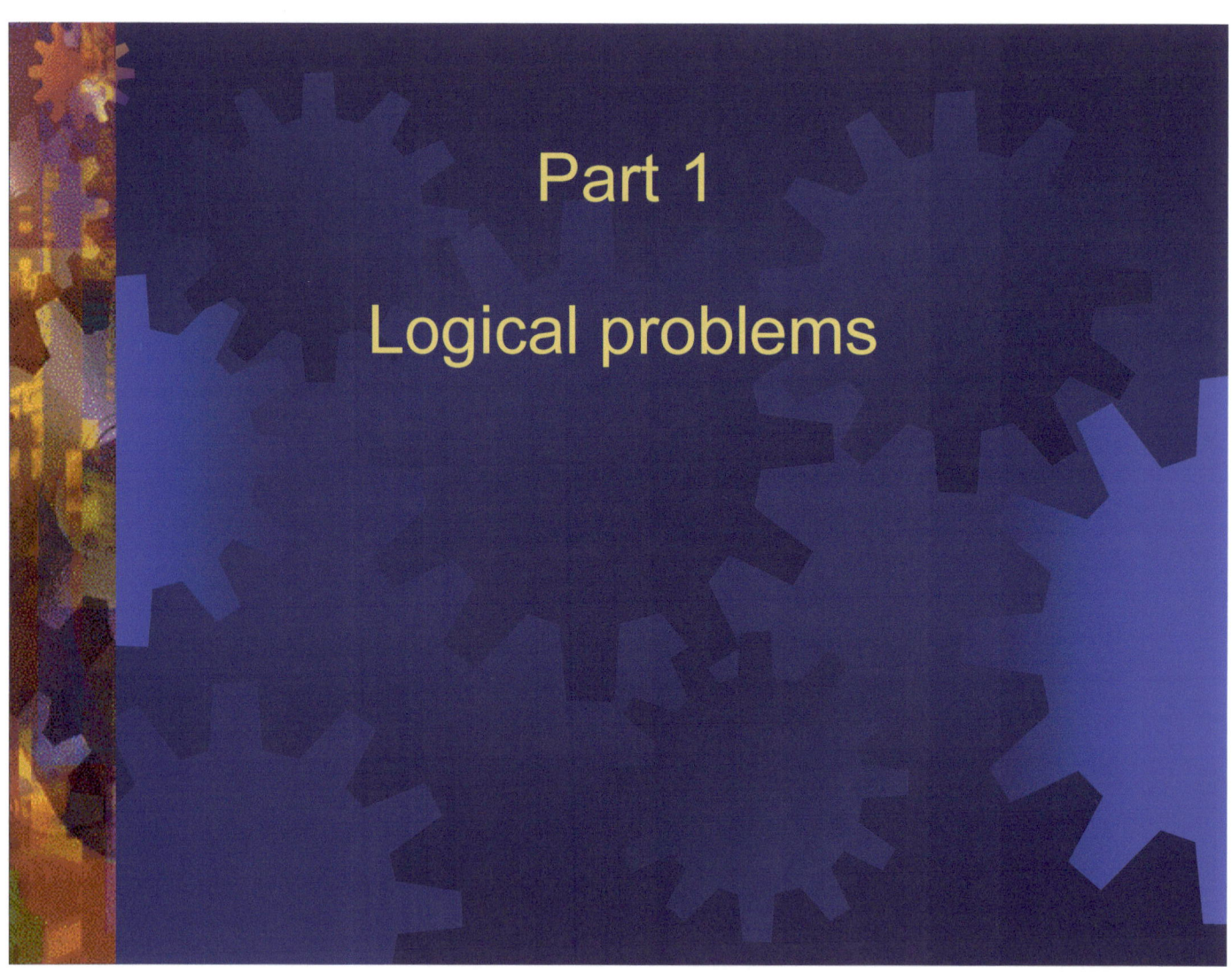

Problem 1

- One water lily bloomed on a lake on the first day of summer. Every day after that the number of blooming lilies doubled.
- On the 20th day the entire lake was covered by lilies.
- On what day was one half of the lake covered?

Answer

- Let's start from the last day. In the previous day the number of lilies was 2 times as small. That means one half of the lake was covered on the 19th day.

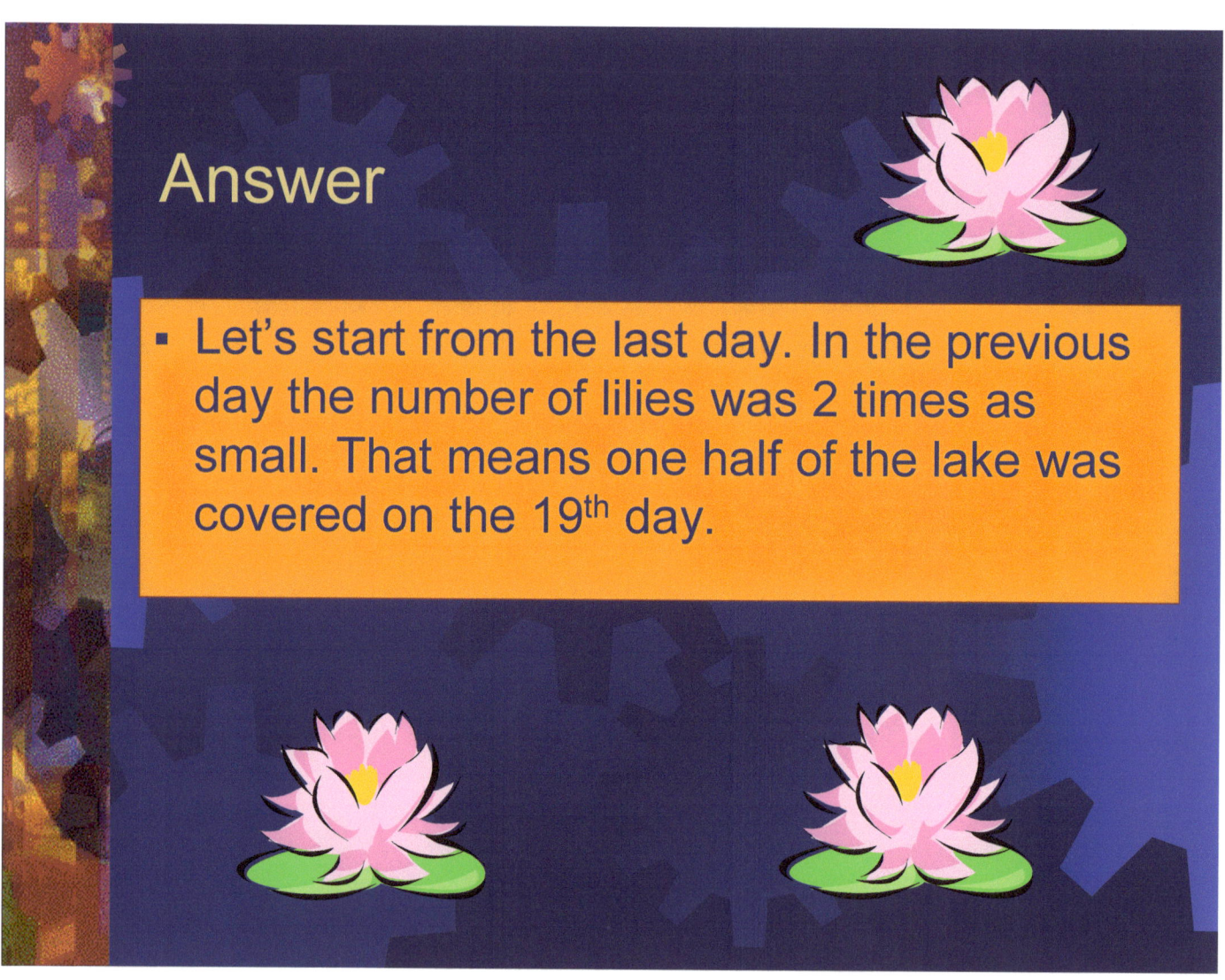

Problem 2

- In some month three Wednesdays fell on even dates.
- What day of week was the 18th of that month?

Answer

- The first Wednesday could only be the 2nd day of the month; the second one, the 16th, and the third one, the 30th. Otherwise the month would have more than 31 days.

- That means that the 18th day of the month was Friday.

Problem 3

7	31
8	28 or 29
5	31
5	30
3	31
4	30

- Guess the rule and fill in the empty cells.

Answer

7	31 January
8	28 or 29 February
5	31 March
5	30 April
3	31 May
4	30 June
4	31 July
6	31 August
9	30 September

- The left column lists the number of letters in the names of the months: the right one, the number of days in those months .

Problem 4

- Can you continue the row:

O; T; T; F; F; S; …

Problem 5

- Can you move the knight on a chessboard, so that it starts in the lower left corner, ends in the upper right corner, and visits each square exactly once?

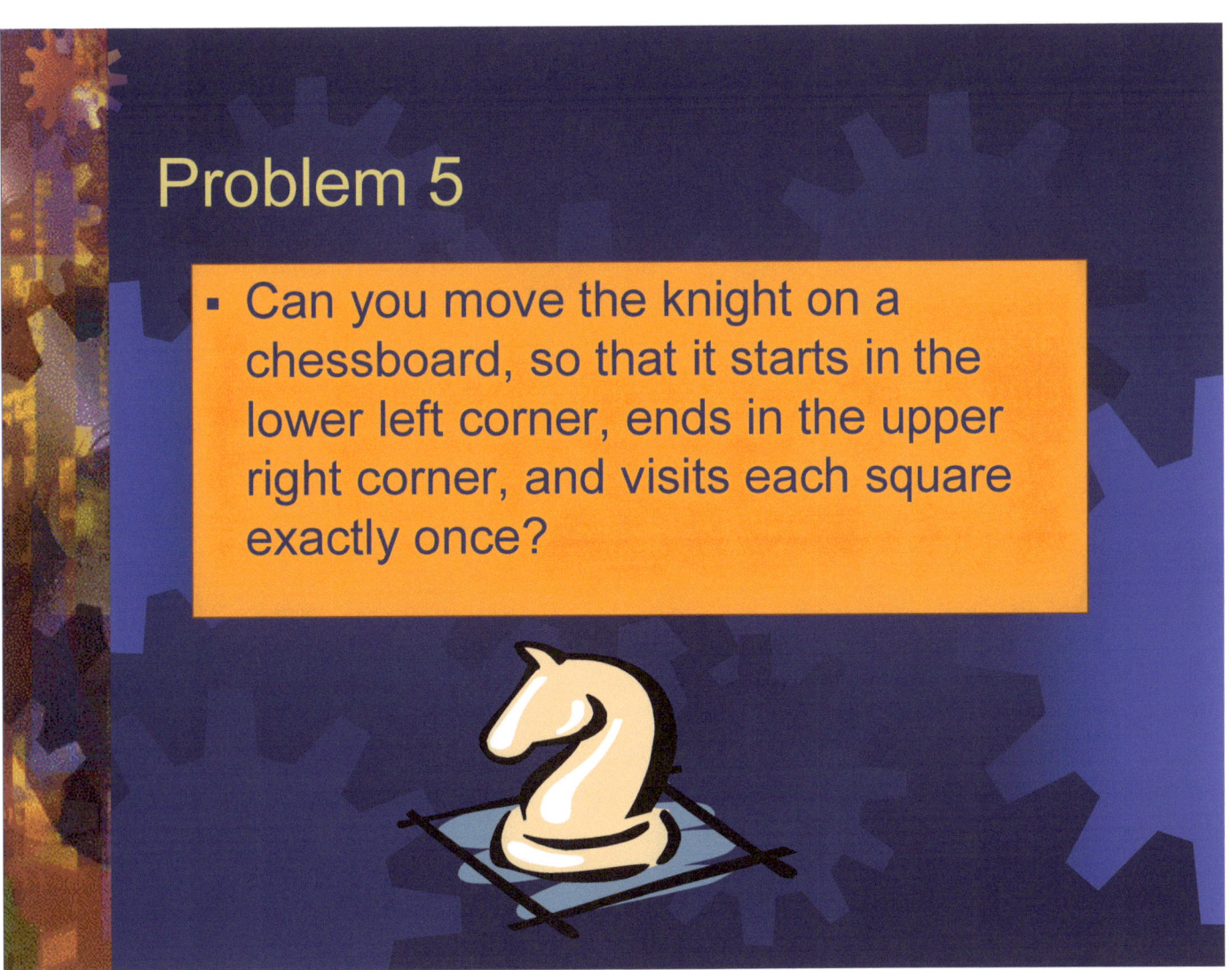

Answer

- Let's start from a white cell. After the first move we get to a black cell, after the second one, to a white one and so on. To get to the 64-th cell we have to perform 63 moves. That means we will end up in a black cell, which is a contradiction.

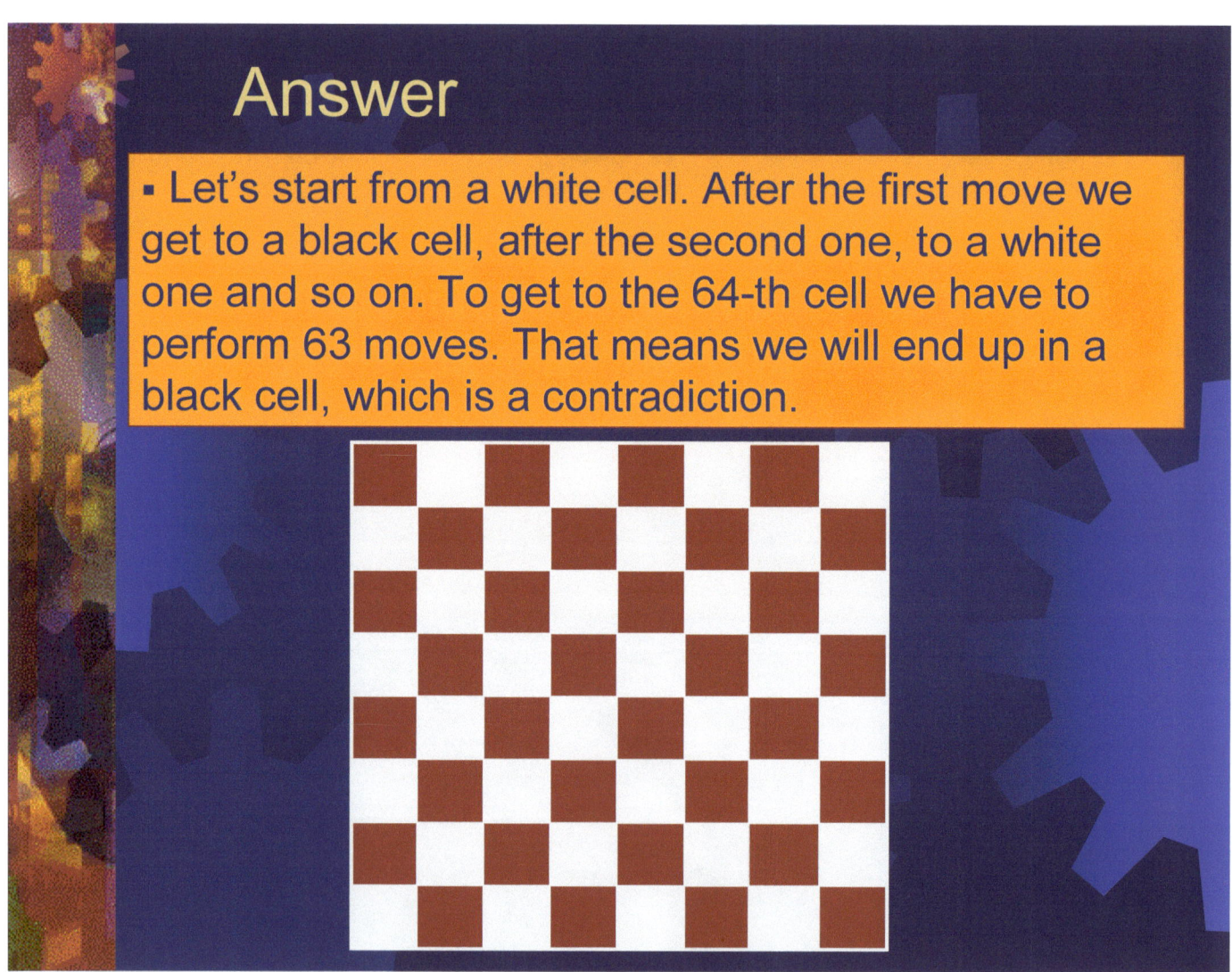

Problem 6

- Can one fill a 5x5 square with numbers, so that all column sums are positive and all row sums are negative?

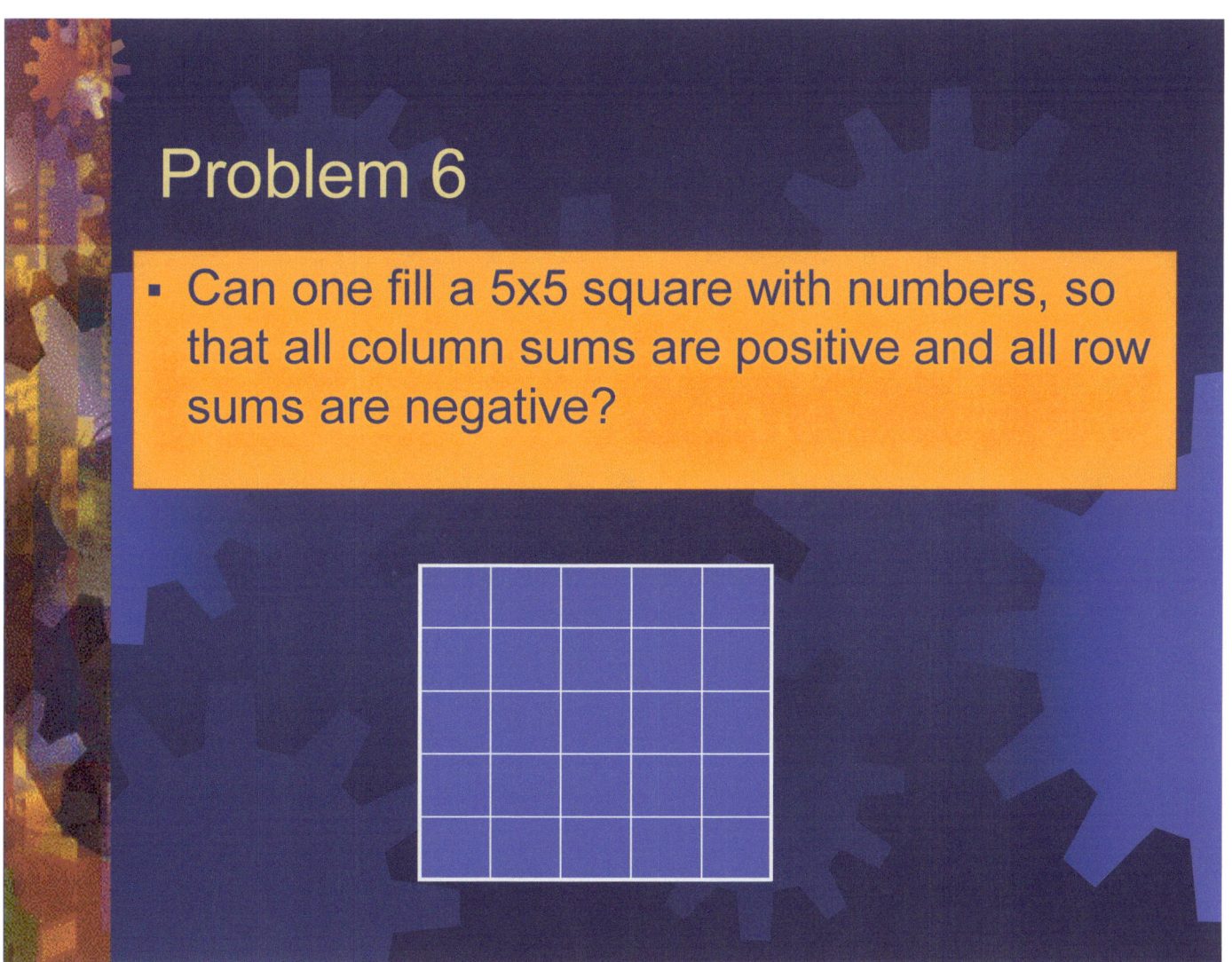

Answer

- Let us prove that it is impossible.
- Suppose we want to calculate the total sum. If we try to add cells column by column we get a negative result. But if we try to add cells raw by raw we get a positive result. That is a contradiction.

Problem 7

- There are three cans that can hold 14 gallons, 9 gallons, and 5 gallons of milk, respectively. The first one is full of milk, the other two are empty.
- How can you split the milk into two equal parts? You can only use these three cans.

Answer

- Let us use the following system of abbreviation.
- "3 → 1; 2, 8, 4." means, "Pour milk from can #3 to can #1. After you do that, the first can will hold 2 gallons of water, the second one, 8 gallons, and the third one, 4 gallons." You start with 14 gallons in the first can.

- Start: 14, 0, 0.
- 1 → 2; 5, 9, 0.
- 2 → 3: 5, 4, 5.
- 3 → 1: 10, 4, 0.
- 2 → 3: 10, 0, 4.
- 1 → 2: 1, 9, 4.
- 2 → 3: 1, 8, 5.
- 3 → 1: 6, 8, 0
- 2 → 3; 6, 3, 5.
- 3 → 1: 11, 3, 0.
- 2 → 3: 11, 0, 3.
- 1 → 2: 2, 9, 3.
- 2 → 3: 2, 7, 5.
- 3 → 1: 7, 7, 0.

Problem 8

- There are six numbers:

  1, 2, 3, 4, 5, 6.

- You can add 1 to any two of them simultaneously and repeat this process as many times as you wish.

- Can you make all the numbers equal?

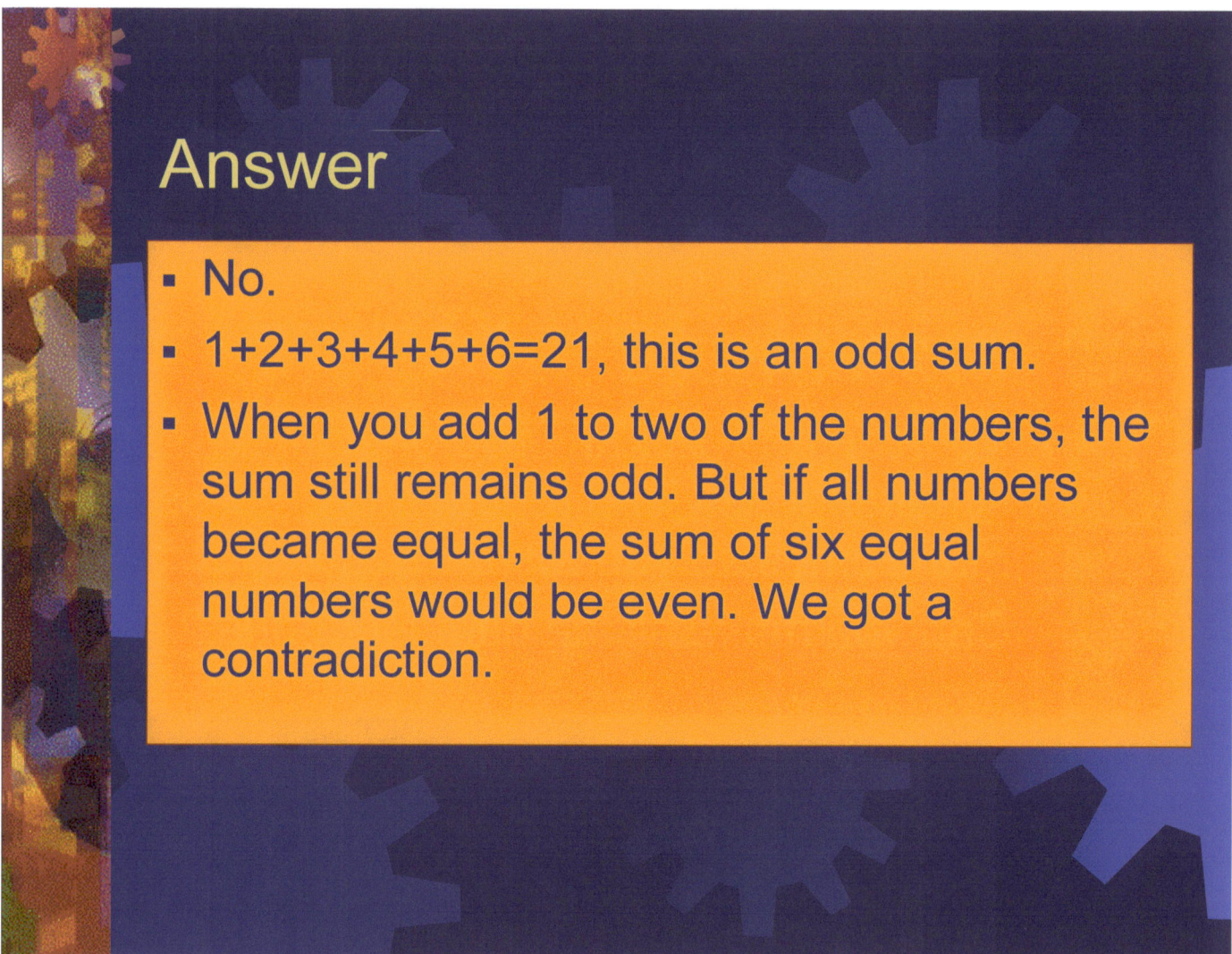

Problem 9

- Three girls ate three pies in three hours.
- How many pies will six girls eat in six hours?

Answer

- **Twelve:**
  - Three girls in one hour eat one pie;
  - Three girls in six hours eat six pies;
  - Six girls in six hours eat twelve pies.

Problem 10

- Guess the rule and continue the row:

  2 3 6 1 8 8 6 4 2 4 …

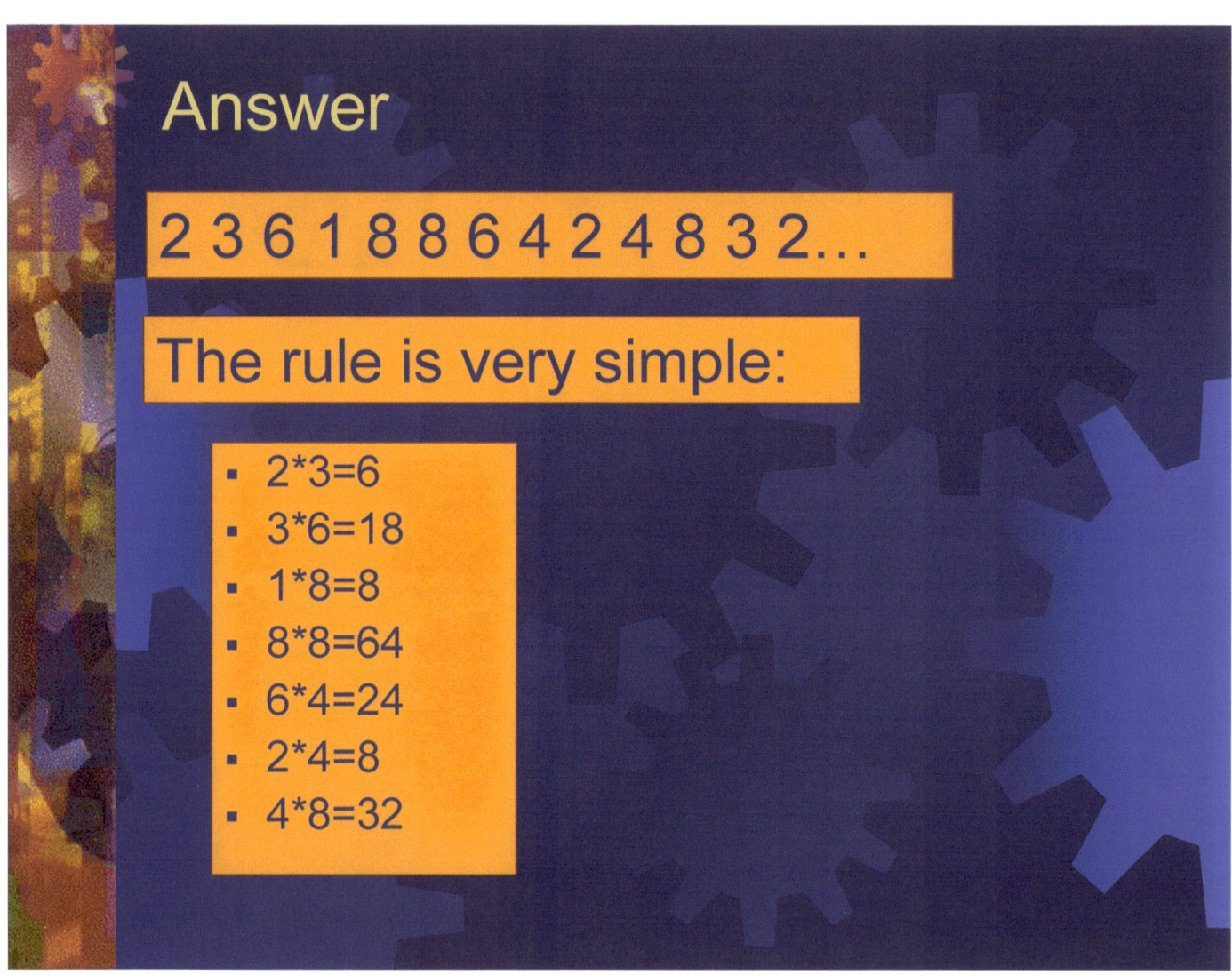

Part 2
Cutting

Problem 1

The figure on the right is composed of three equal squares.

Can you cut it into four equal parts?

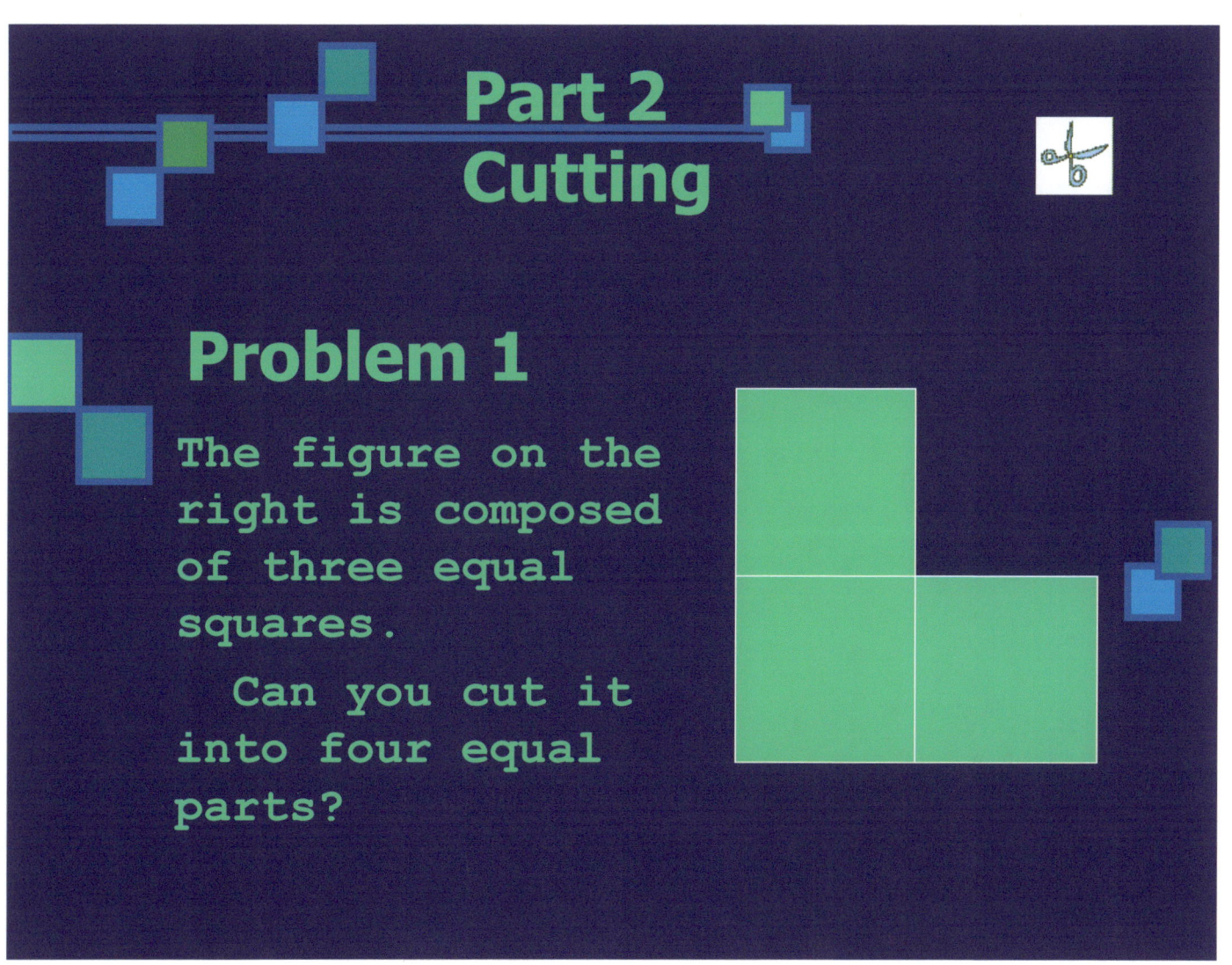

Answer

Cut along the red line.

You will get four equal parts.

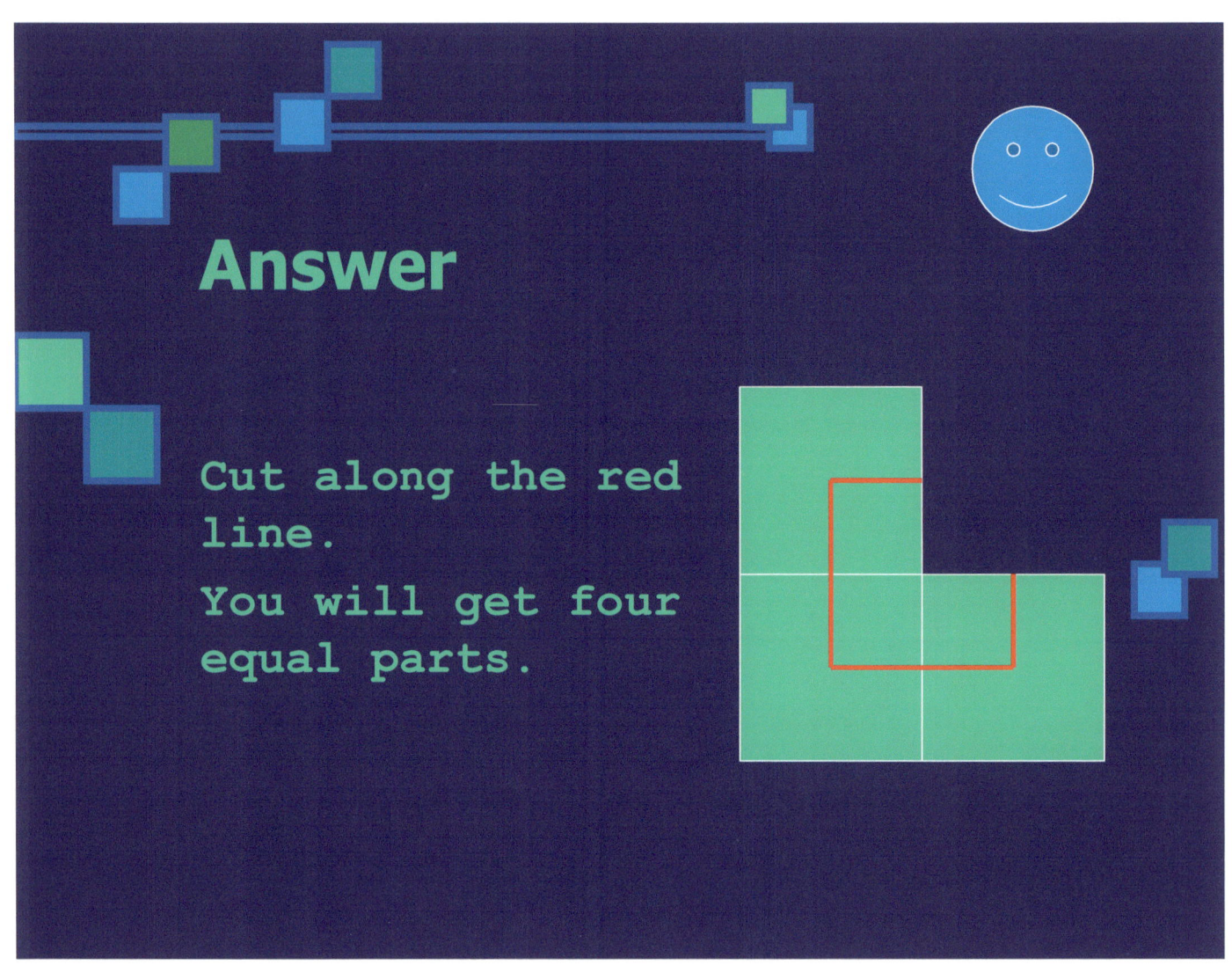

Problem 2

Cut this figure in two peaces and rearrange them to make a square with a square hole inside.

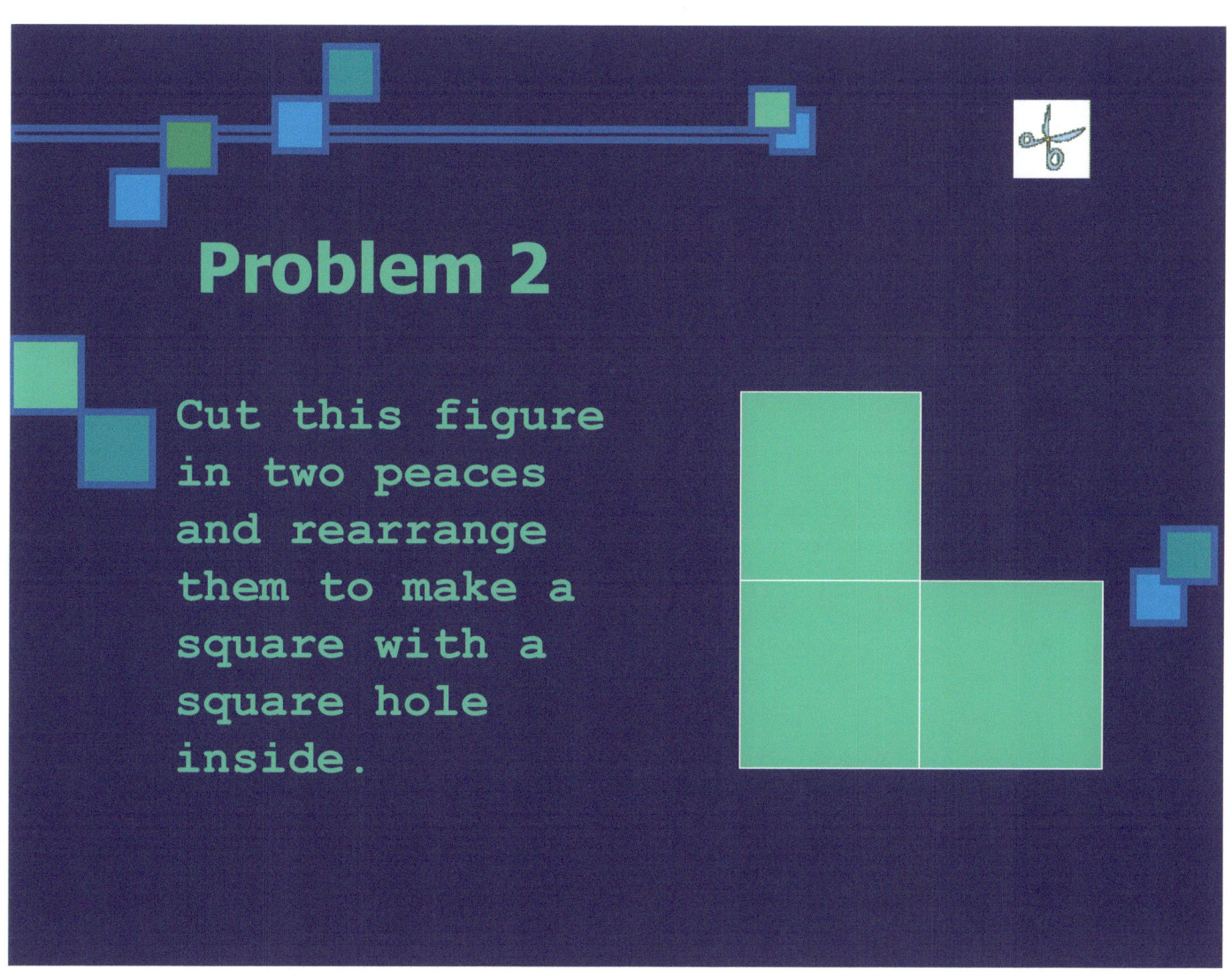

Answer

1. Cut the figure the same way as in Problem 1
2. Move the inner piece to the upper right corner.

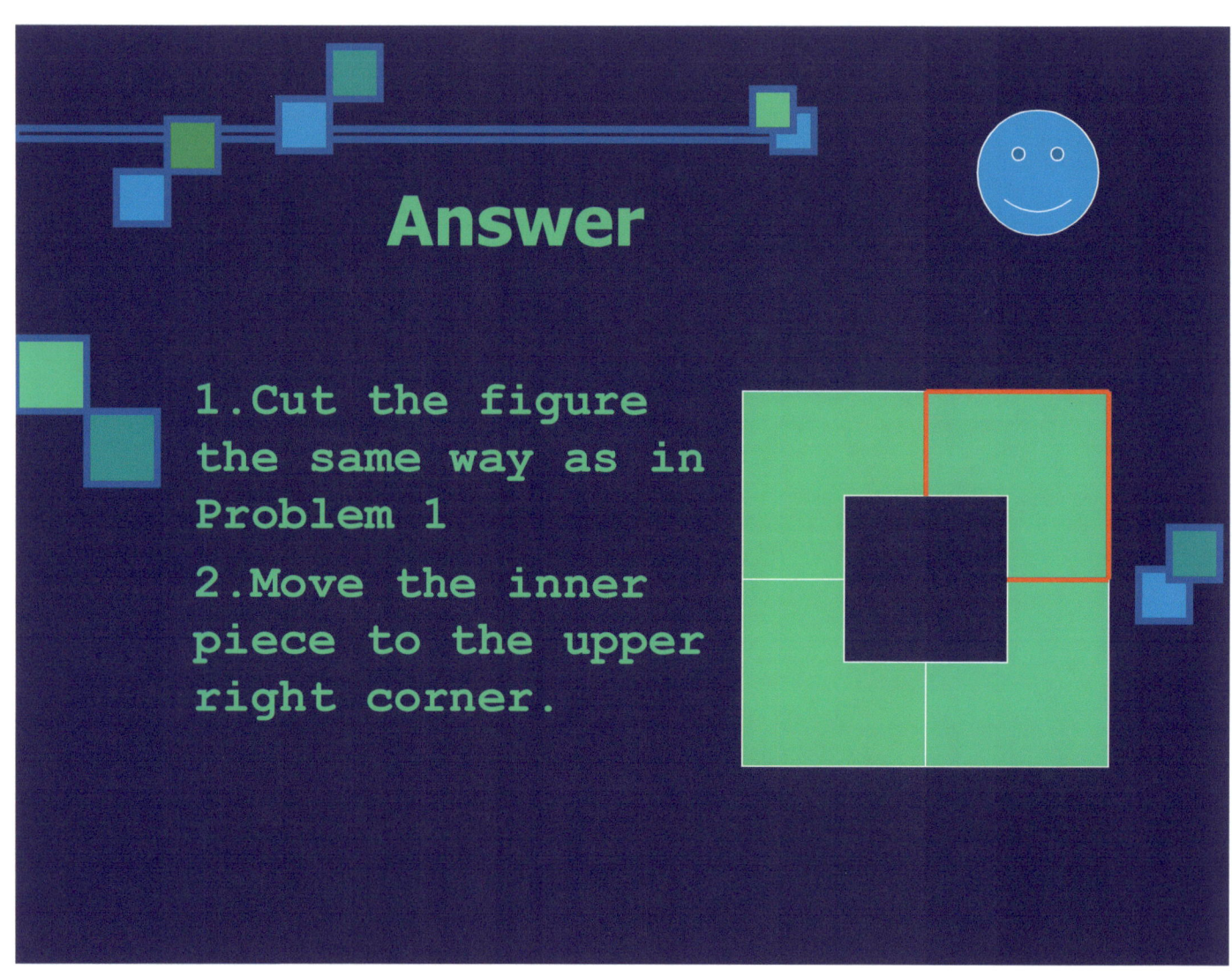

Problem 3

Can you split a square into five equal parts?

Answer

Split it into five equal stripes.

Problem 4

There are seven circles on a rug.

Can you draw three straight lines and cut the rug along these lines to get seven parts with one circle on each part?

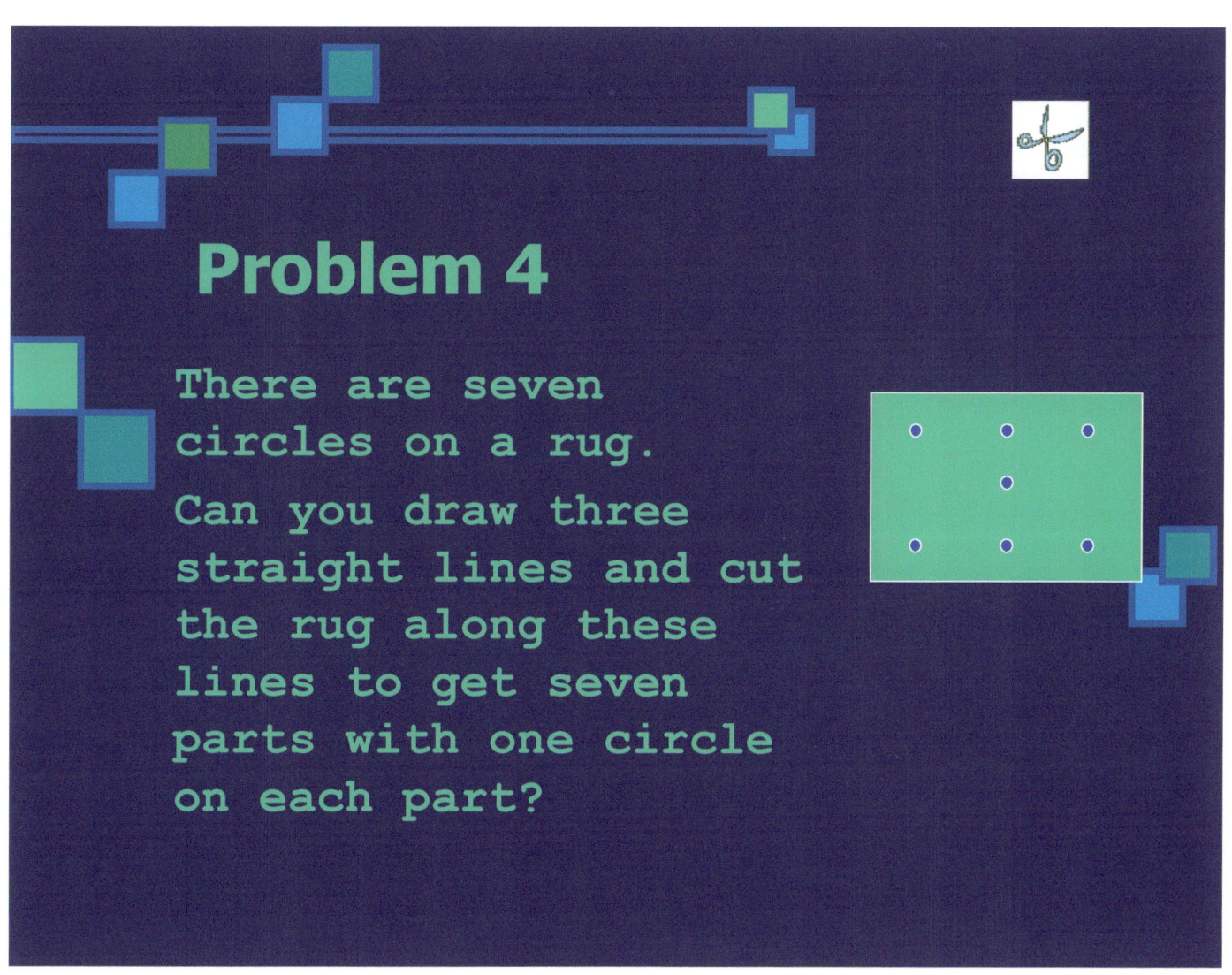

Answer

The three cut lines are shown on the picture.

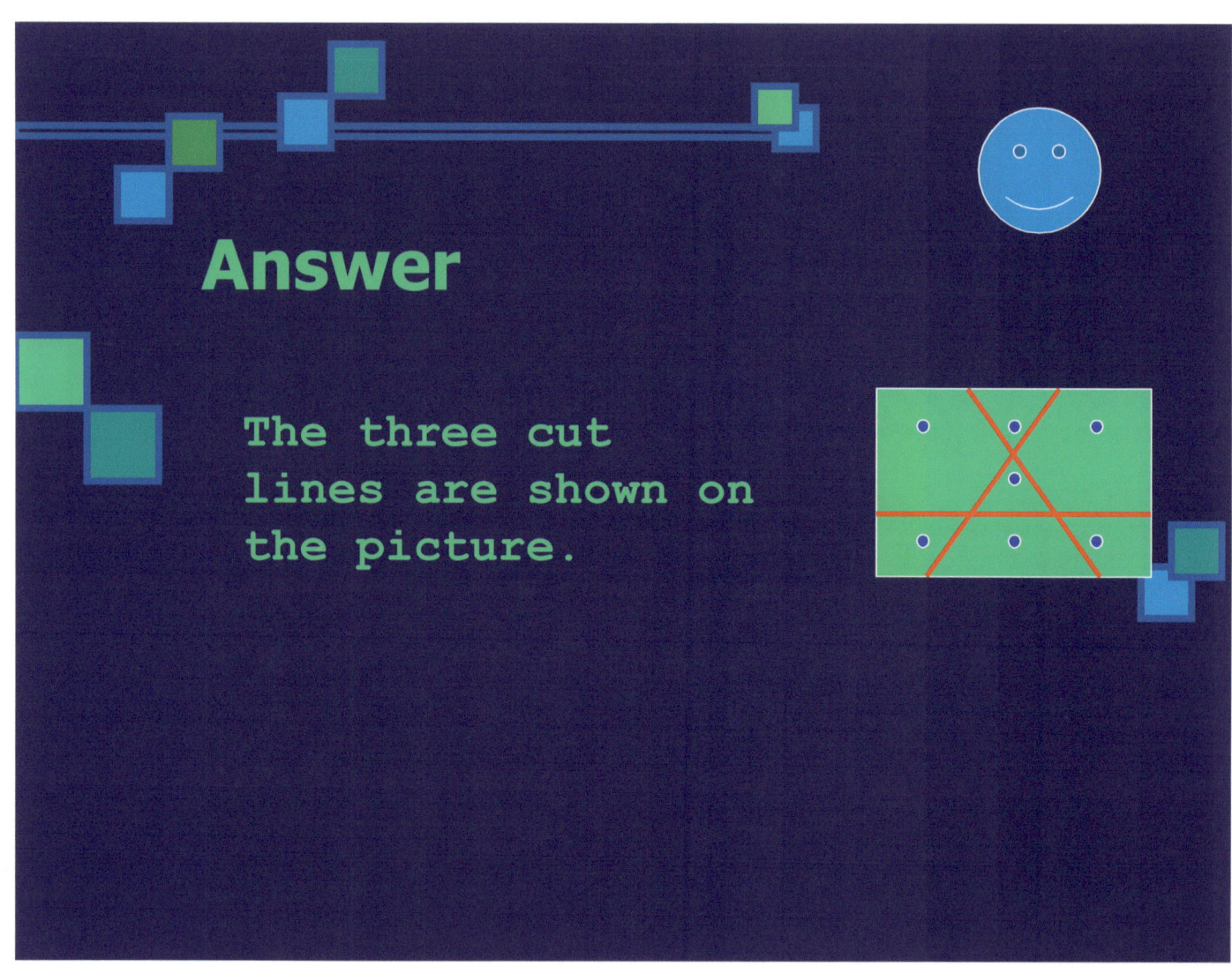

Problem 5

Can you cut arbitrary triangle into three parts and put them together to get a rectangle?

Answer

Draw an altitude in the triangle and make a cut from the vertex to the middle of the altitude. Then cut along the center line of triangle. It is easy to prove that the three parts can be rearranged to make a rectangle.

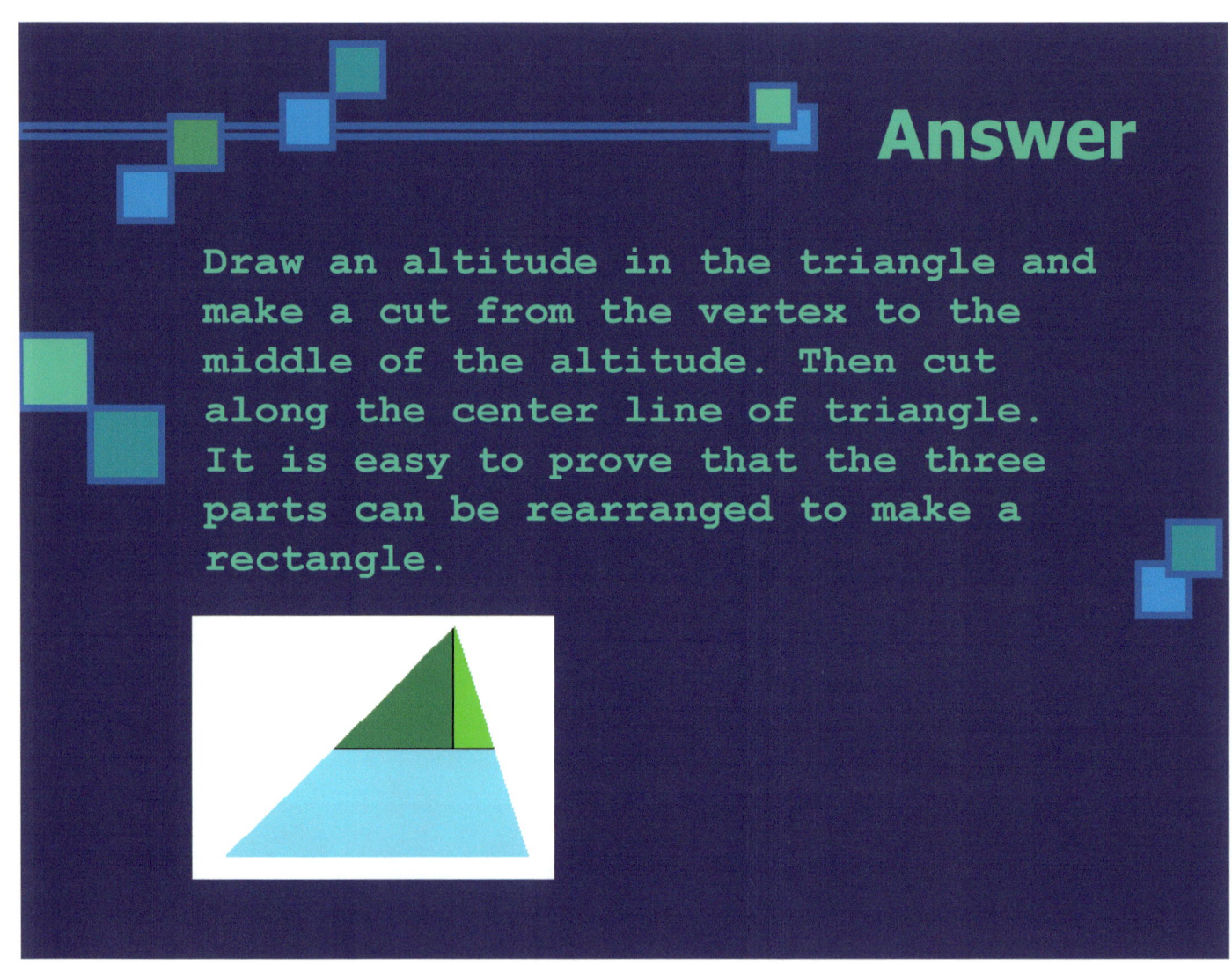

Problem 6

Can you cut the figure below along two straight lines so that the cuts divide it into six parts?

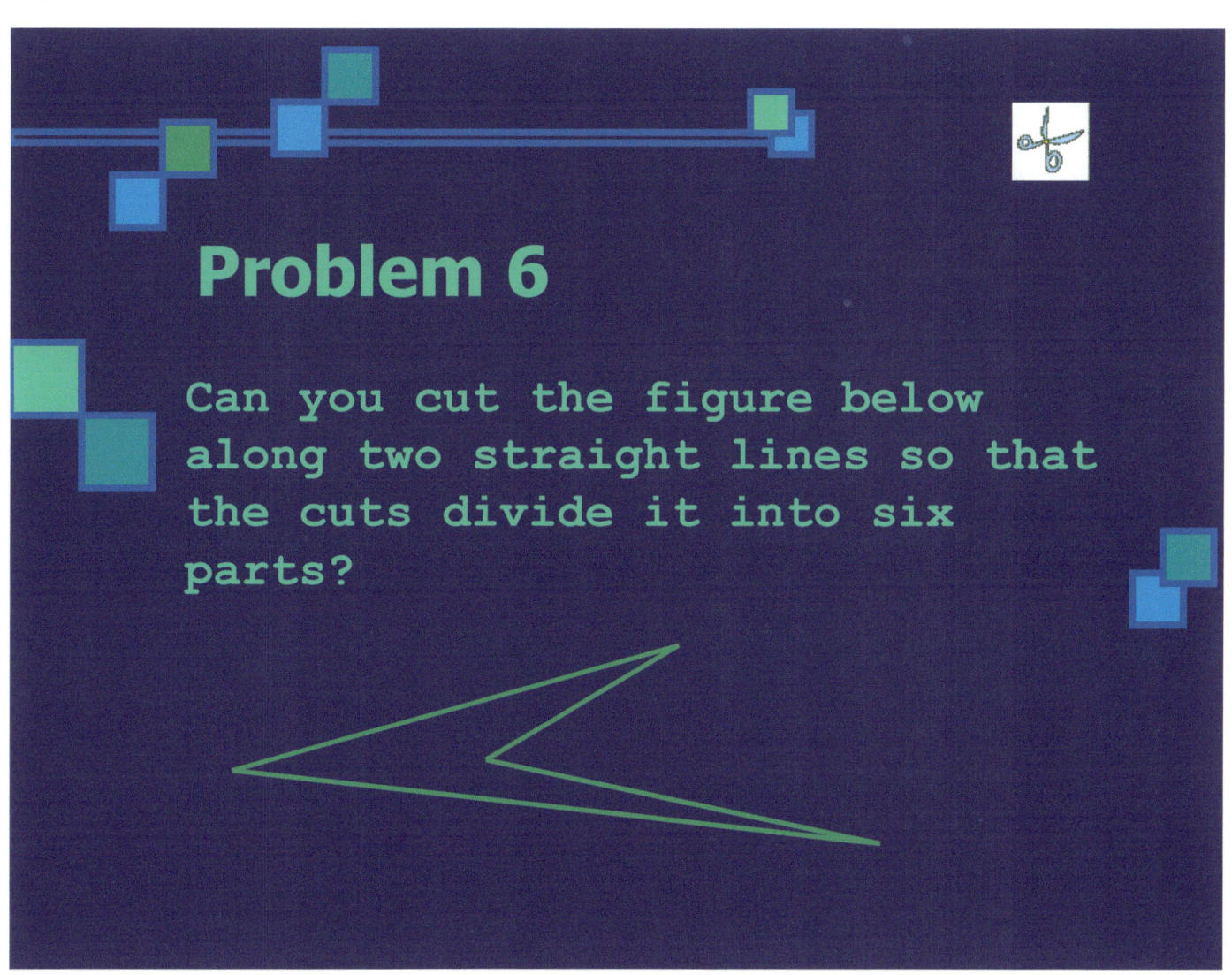

Answer

The two cut lines are shown on the picture.

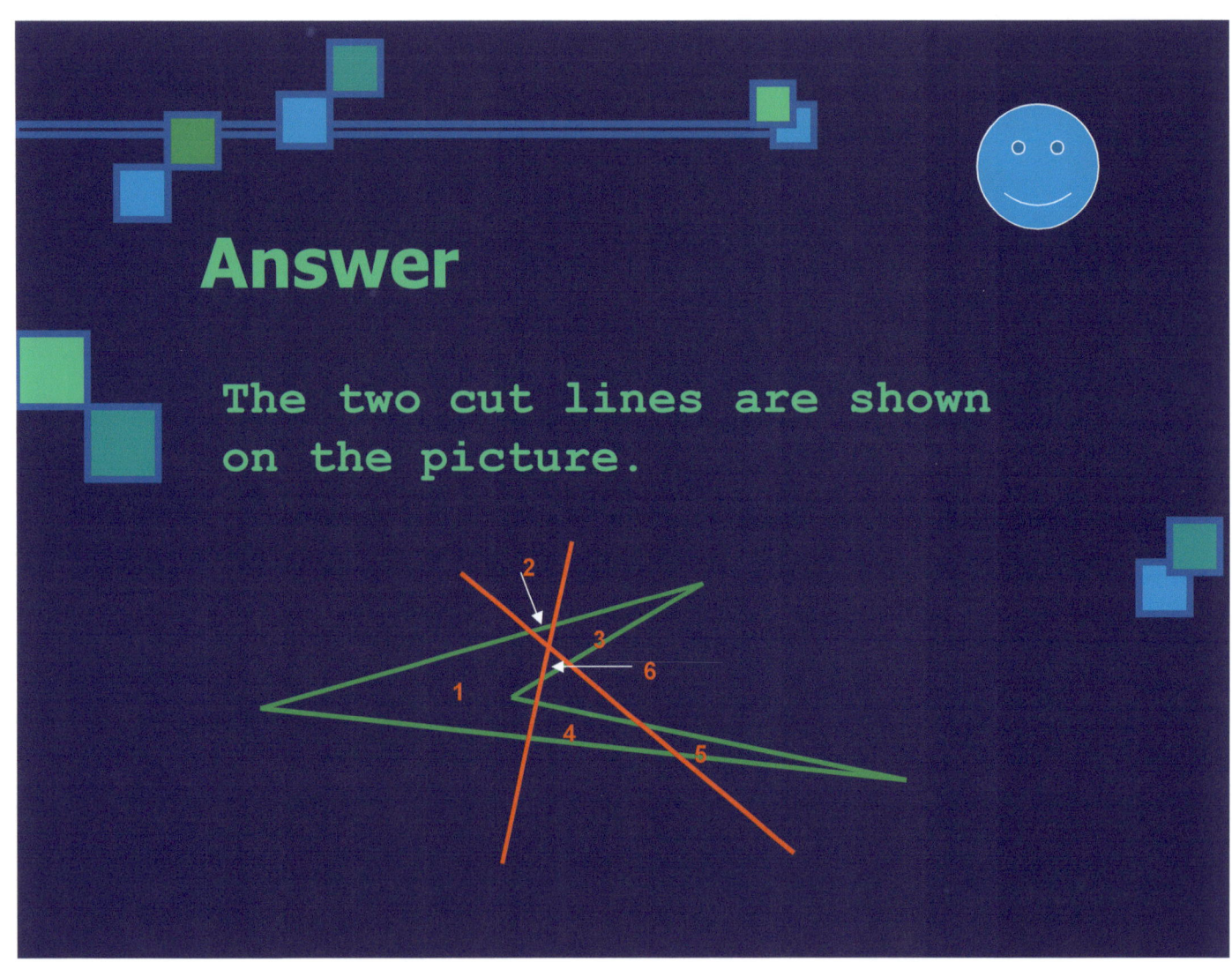

Problem 7

Red lines are drawn on a 6x10 piece of checkered paper.

Can you cut this piece of paper into two parts along red lines and rearrange them to get a 9x7 rectangle with three holes in it?

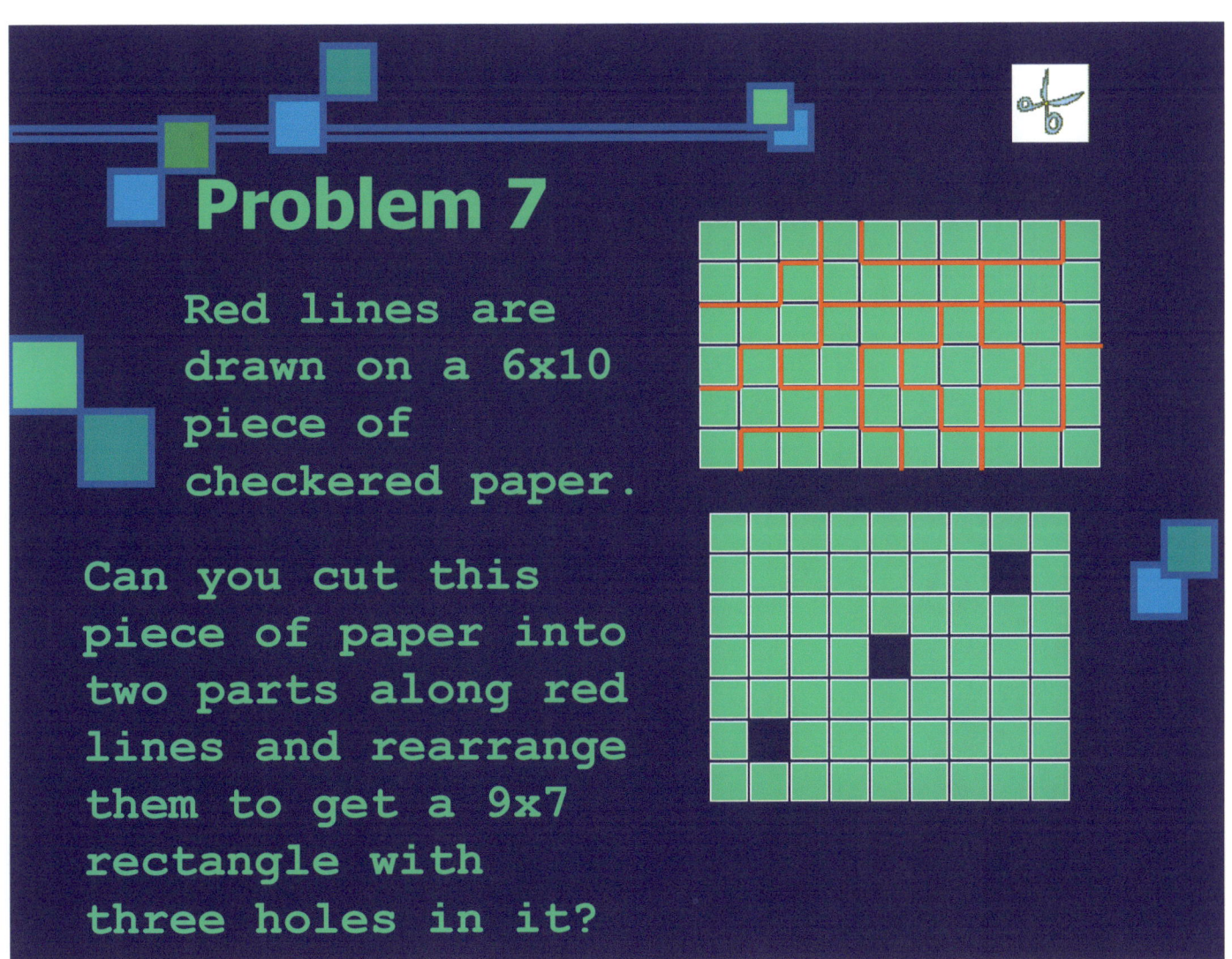

Answer

You should cut along the solid red line.

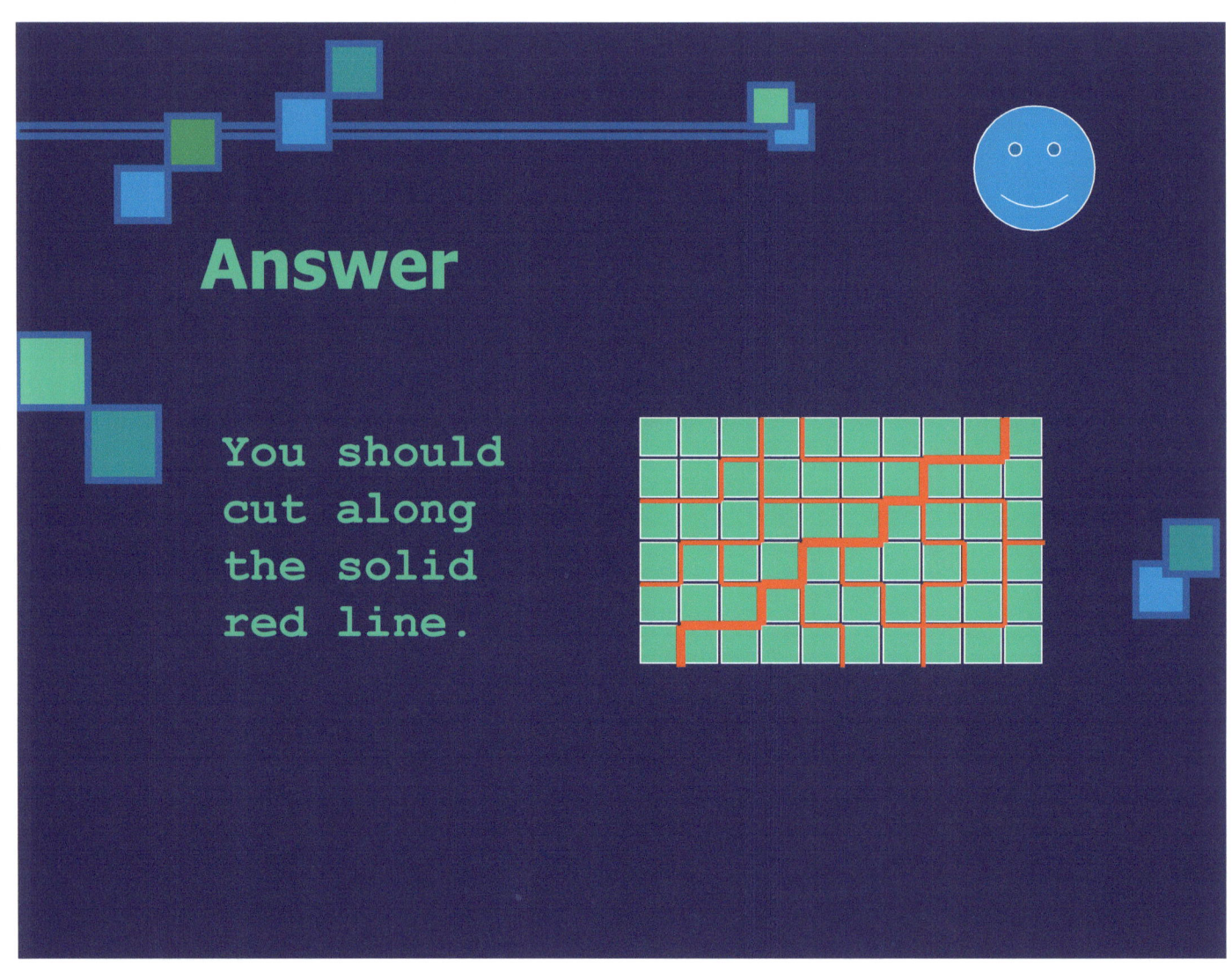

Problem 8

Grandma made a rectangular pie.

Mike insists that he can cut this pie along four straight lines and get 11 pieces of pie (not equal).

How can he do that?

Answer

Mike can cut the pie along the four red lines.

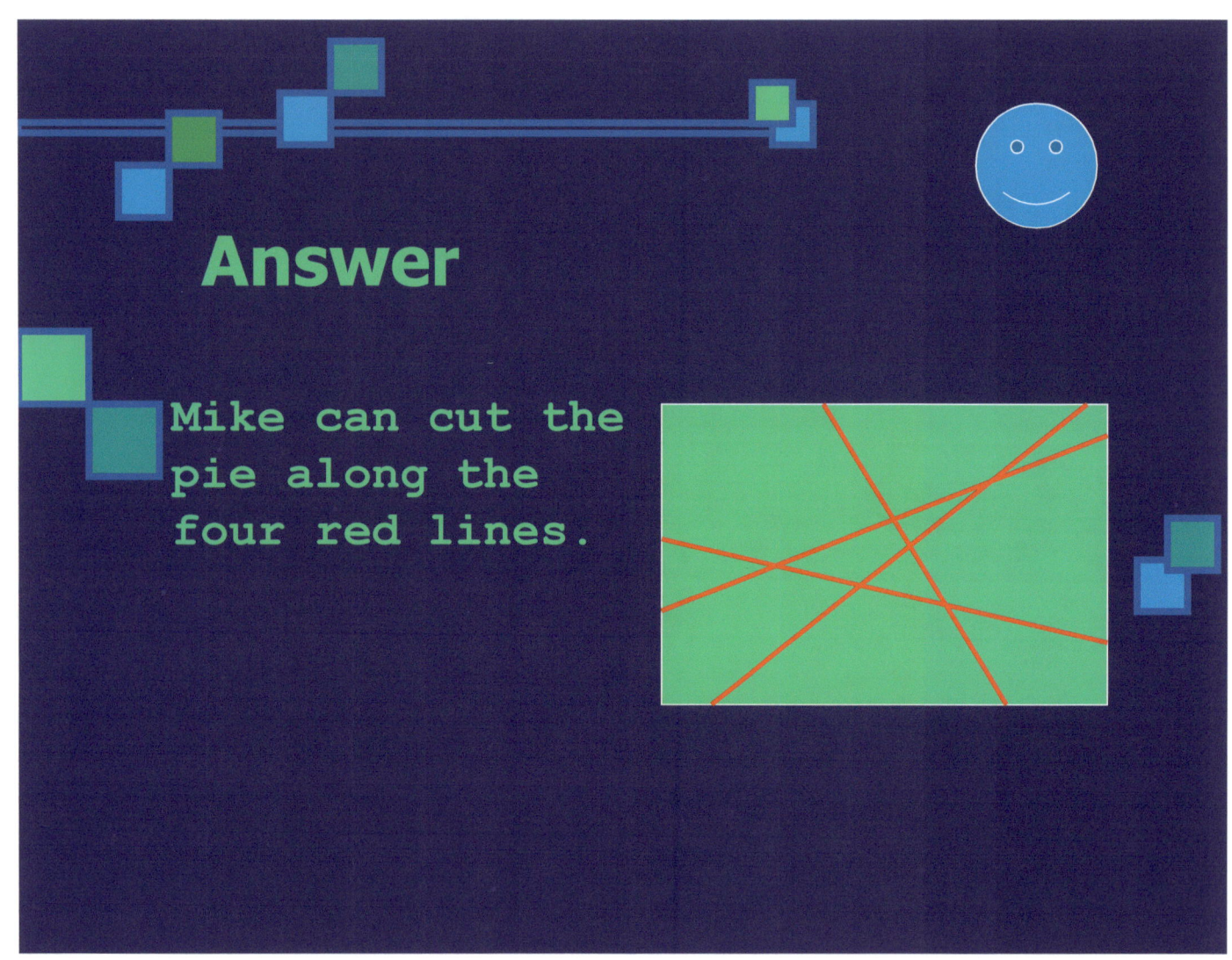

Problem 9

There are two flags on the picture. The width of each flag is twice as big as its height.

Can you cut one flag into four parts and rearrange them to make the other flag?

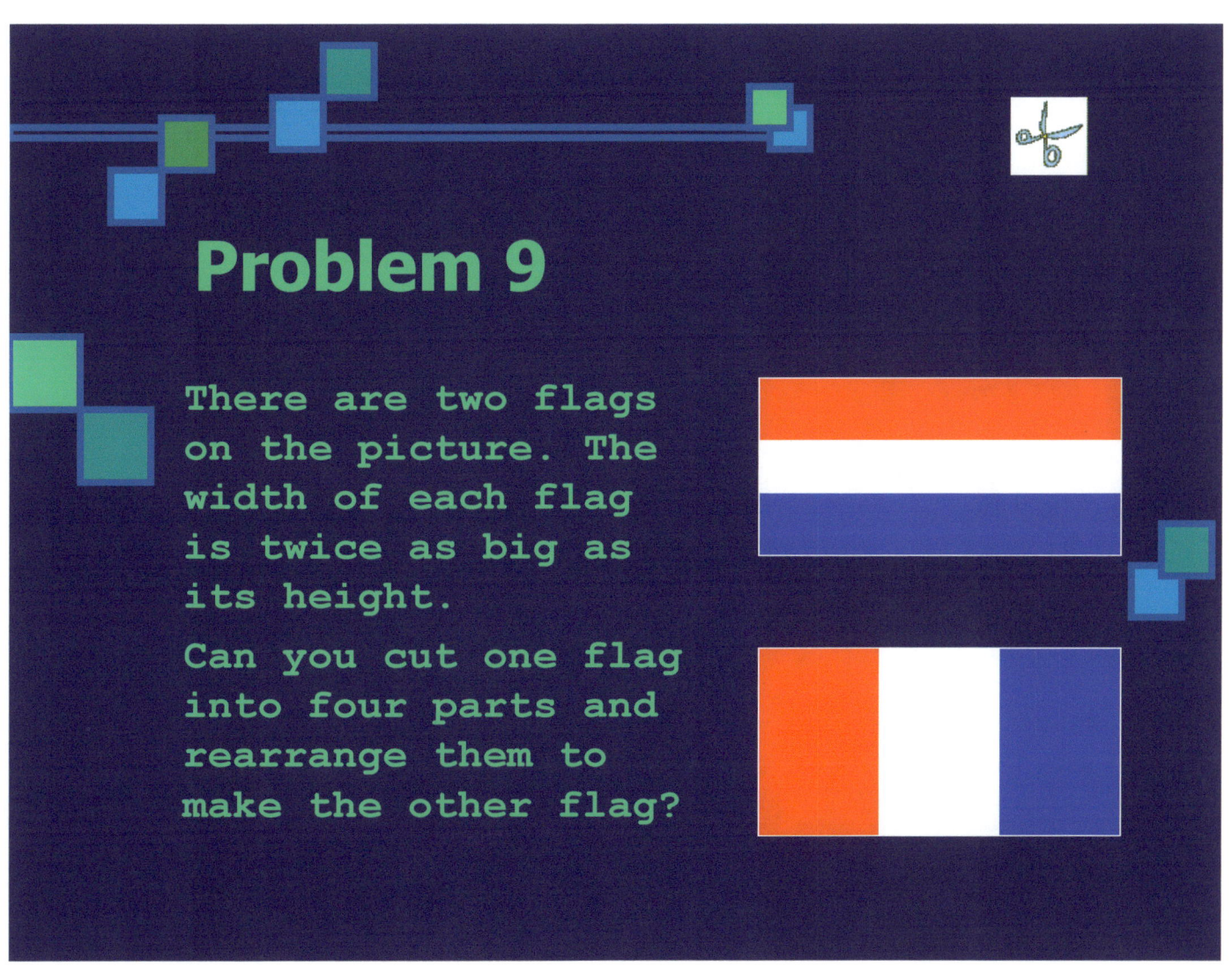

Answer

Cut along the green lines and rearrange the four parts as shown on the picture.

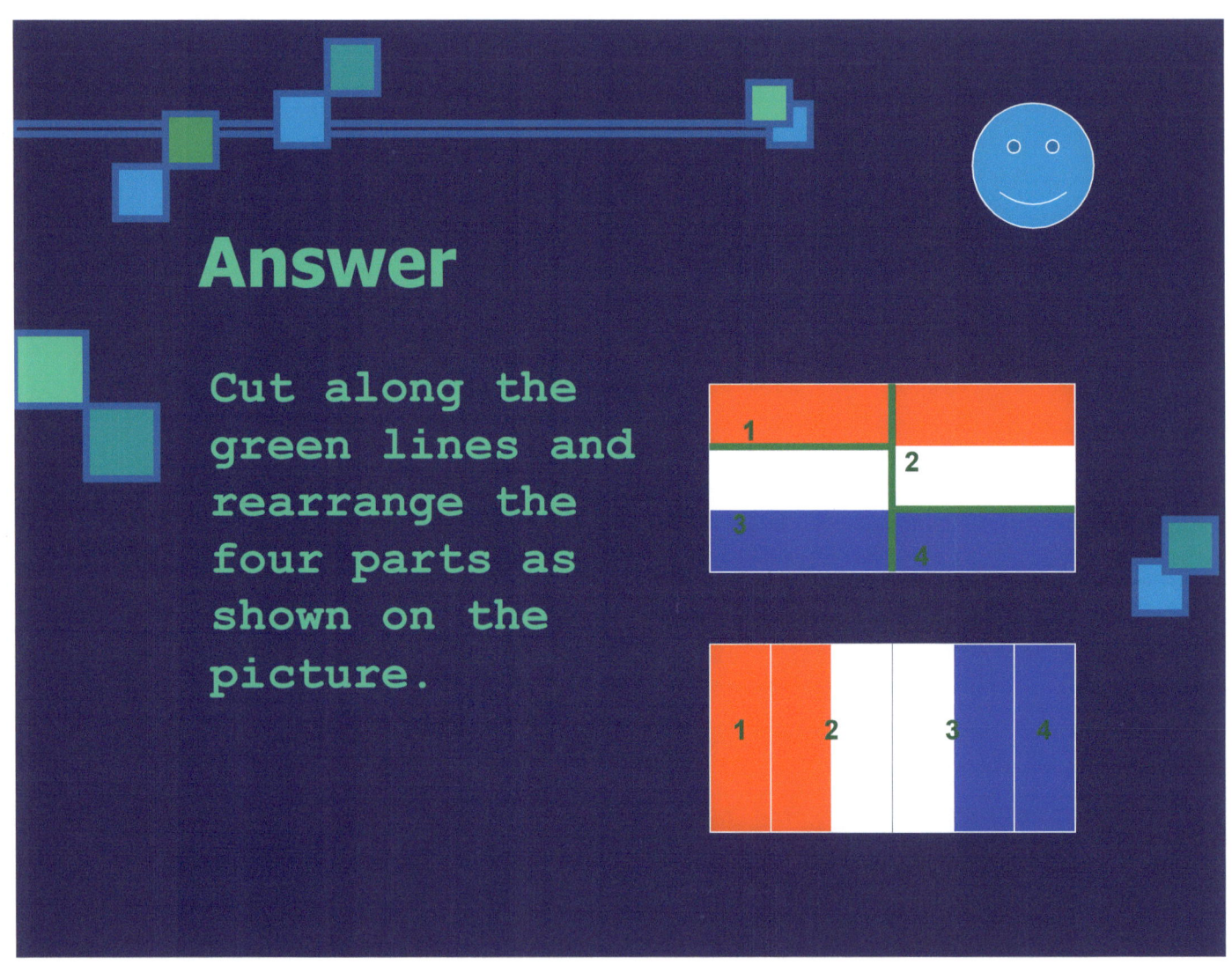

Problem 10

There are two flags on the picture. The width of each flag is one and a half times as big as its height.

Can you cut one flag into four parts and rearrange them into the other flag?

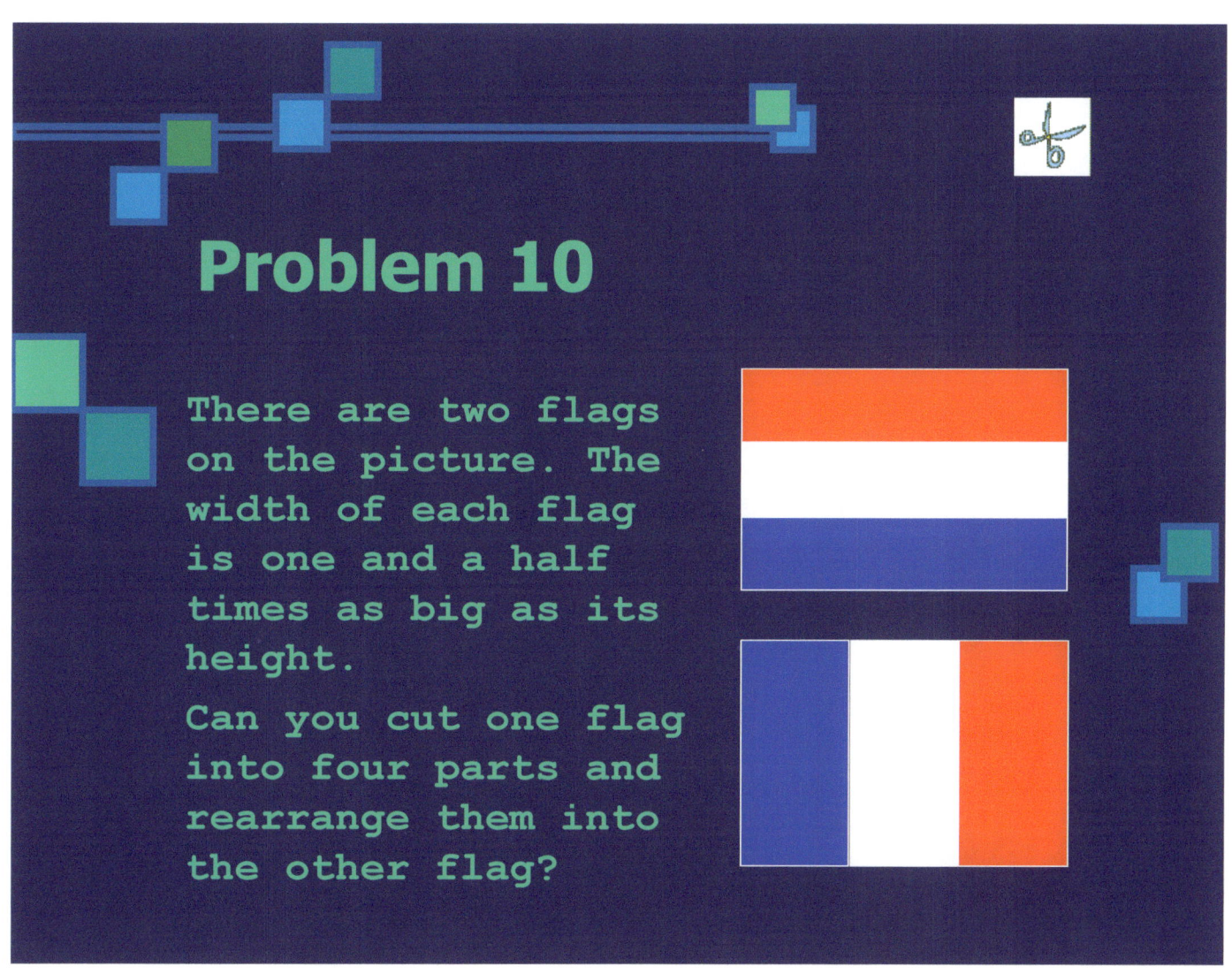

Answer

Cut along the green lines and rearrange the parts as shown on the picture. The dashed lines divide each color strip into six equal parts.

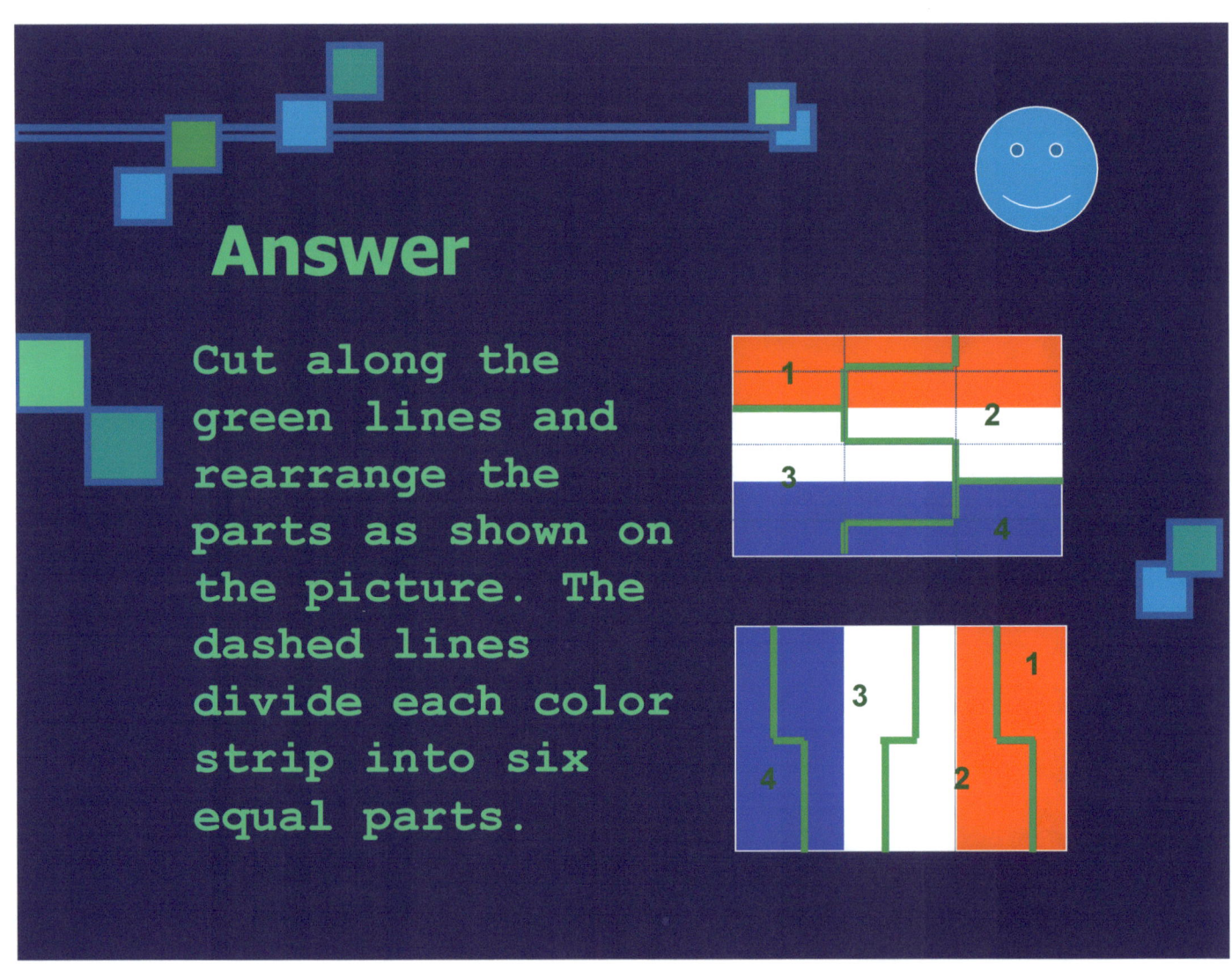

Part 3
Drawing

Problem 1

Can you draw this figure without lifting your pencil? You have to draw each line exactly once.

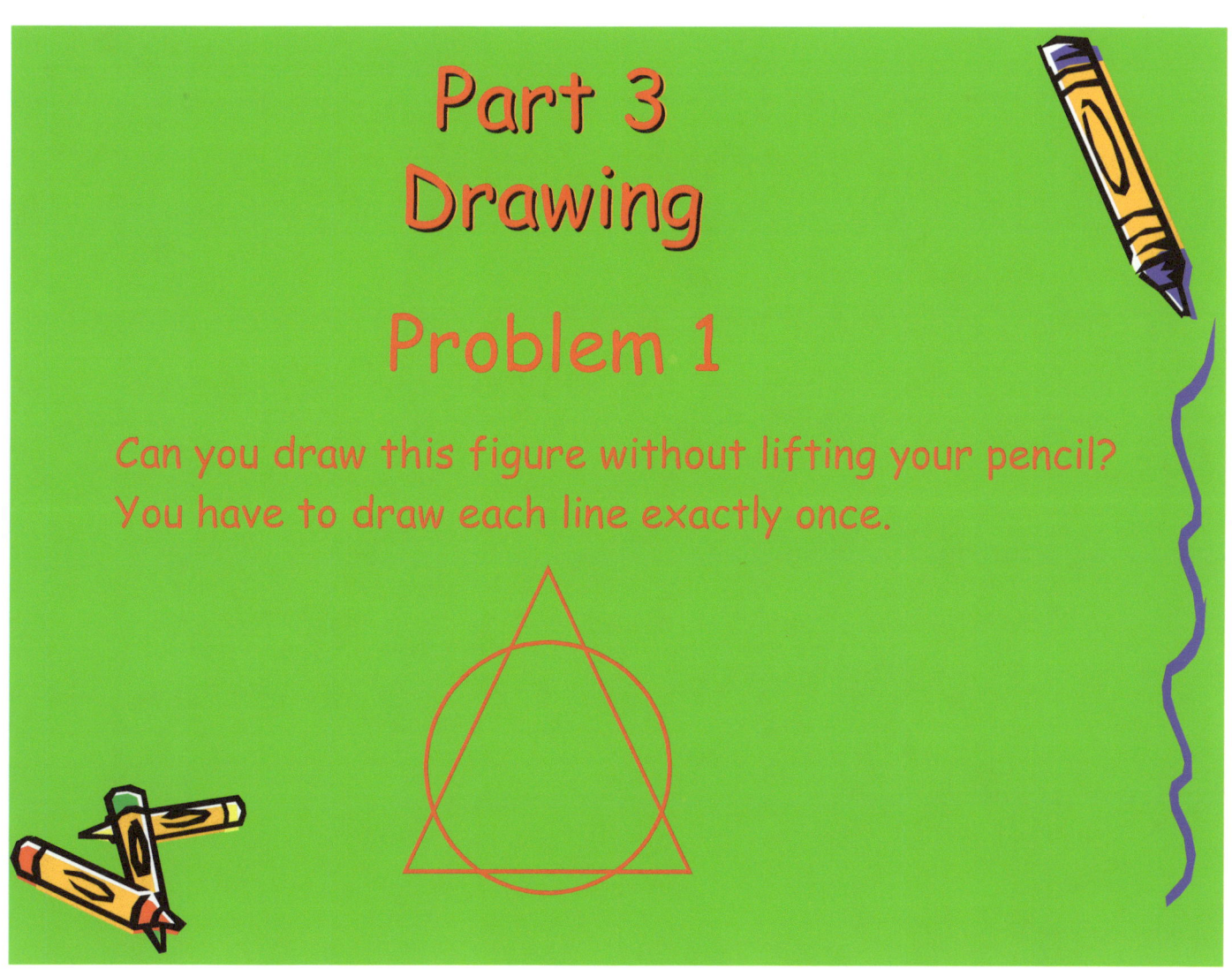

Hint

You can start at point A.

Problem 2

The road map in a magic garden is shown on the picture.

Can Dorothy walk around all roads without walking twice on any path?

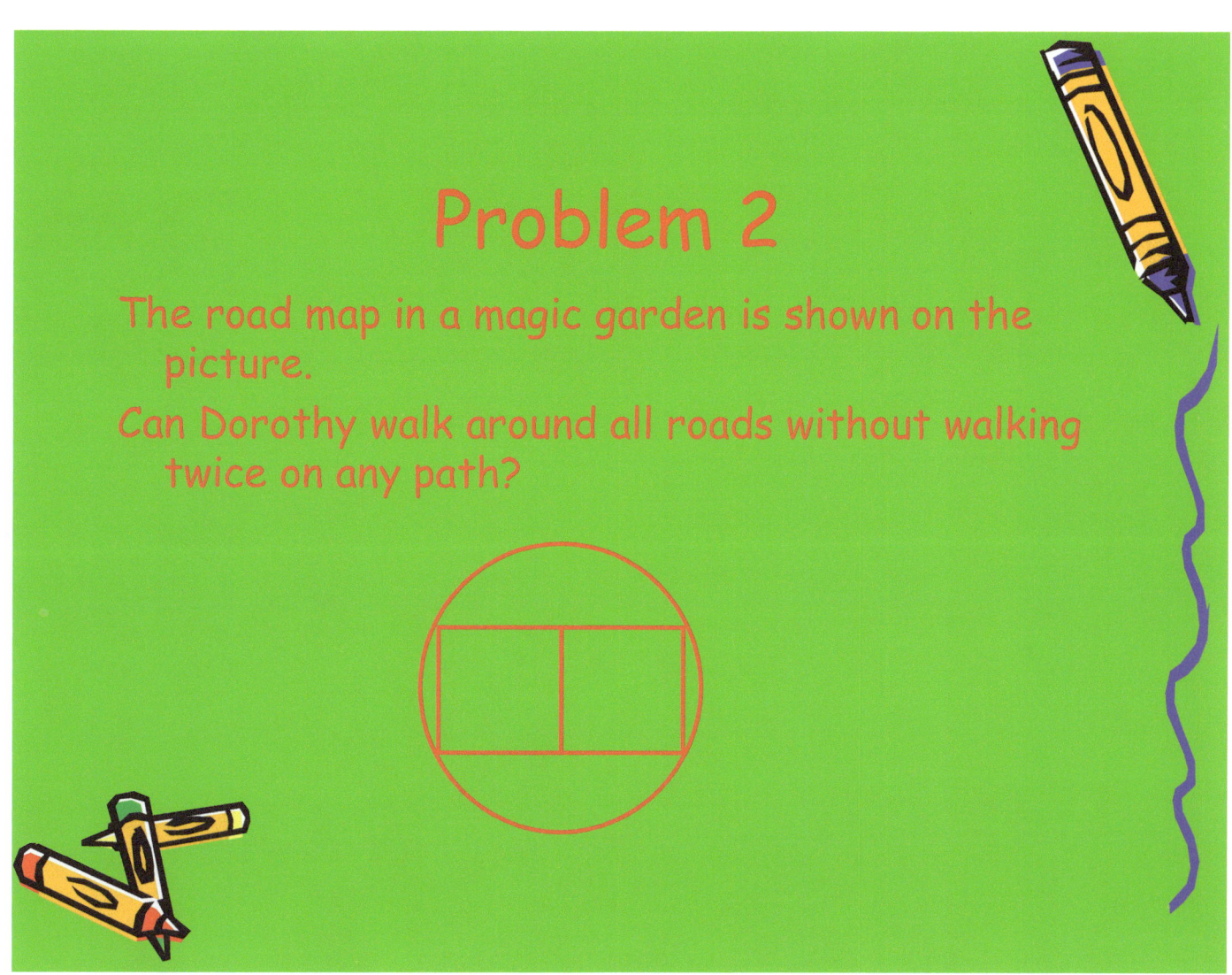

Hint

Dorothy can start at point A.

Problem 3

Can you draw this figure without lifting your pencil?

You have to draw each line exactly once.

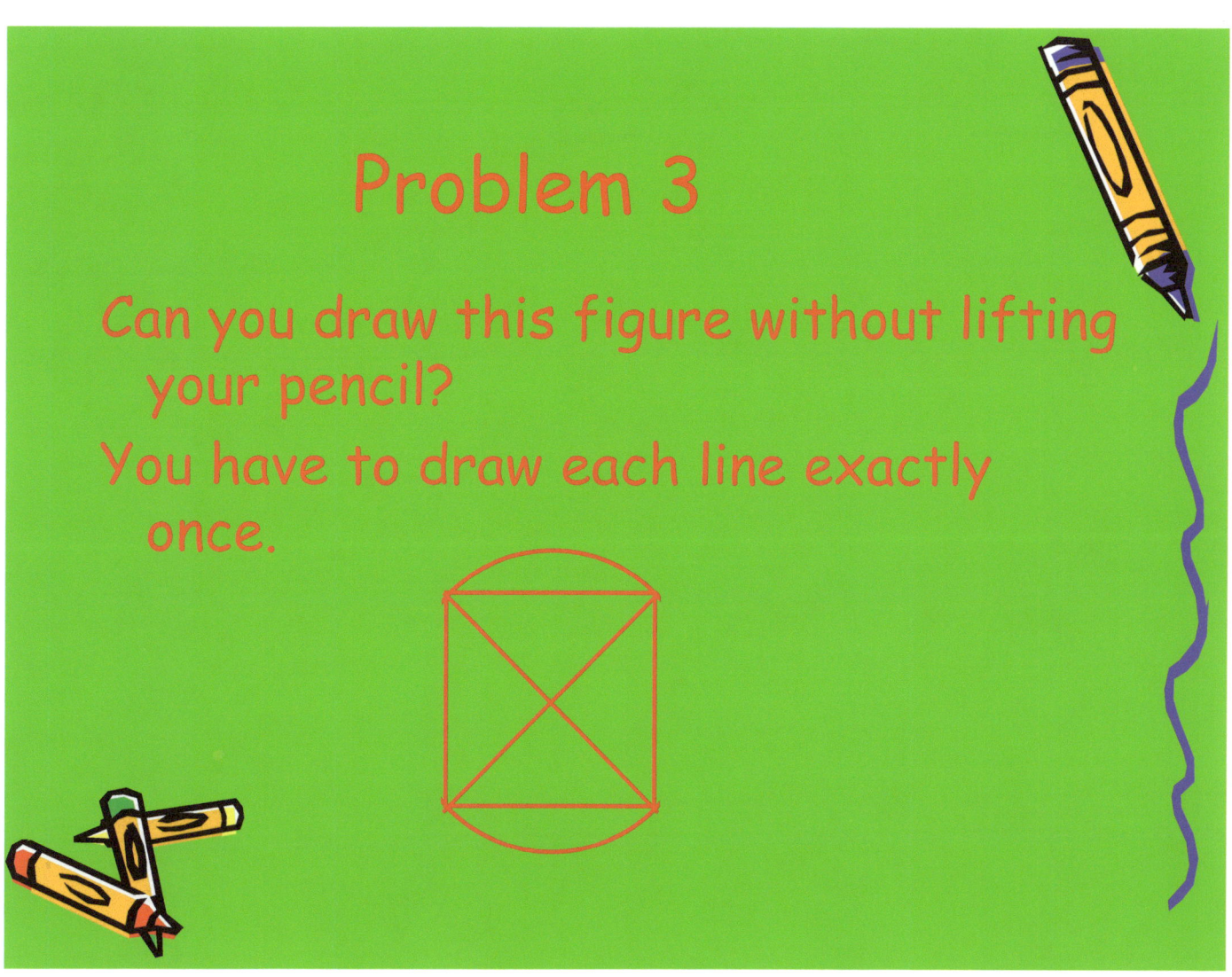

Hint

You can start at point A.

Problem 4

The roads in Mathtown look like a star in a circle.

Can a driver drive through all roads passing each road exactly once?

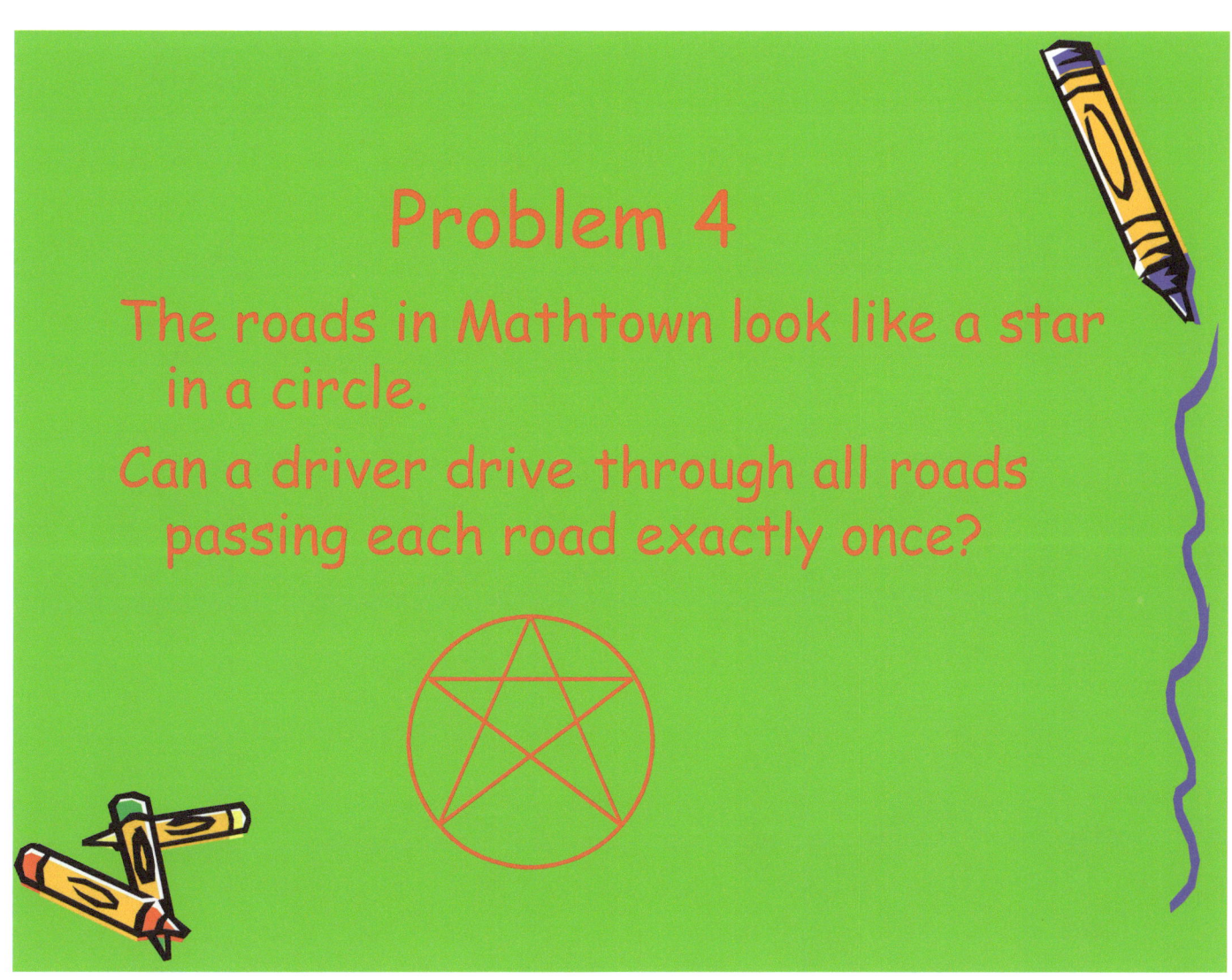

Answer

The driver can start at point A, drive around the circle, and then drive along the star lines.

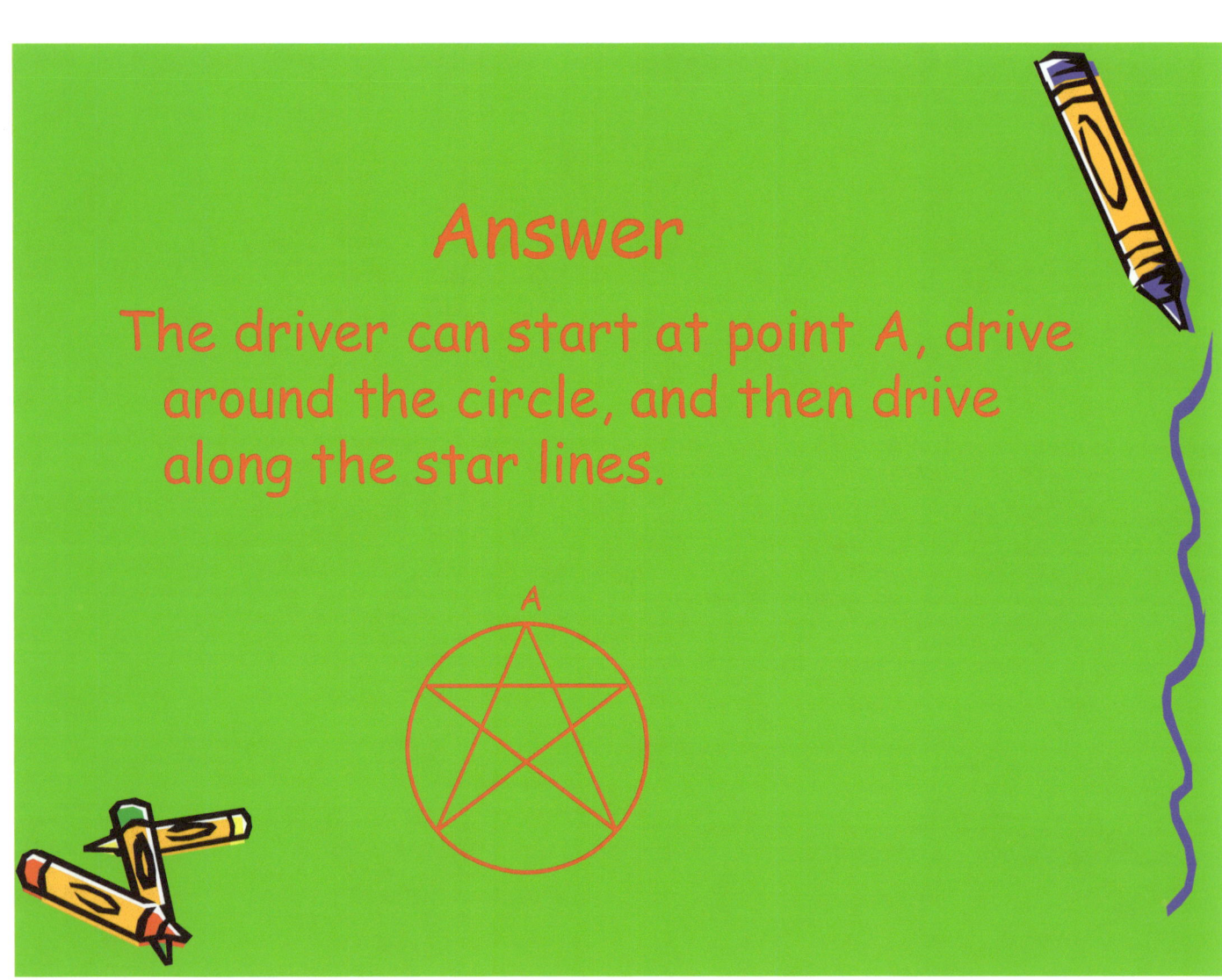

Problem 5

Can you draw this figure without lifting your pencil?

You have to draw each line exactly once.

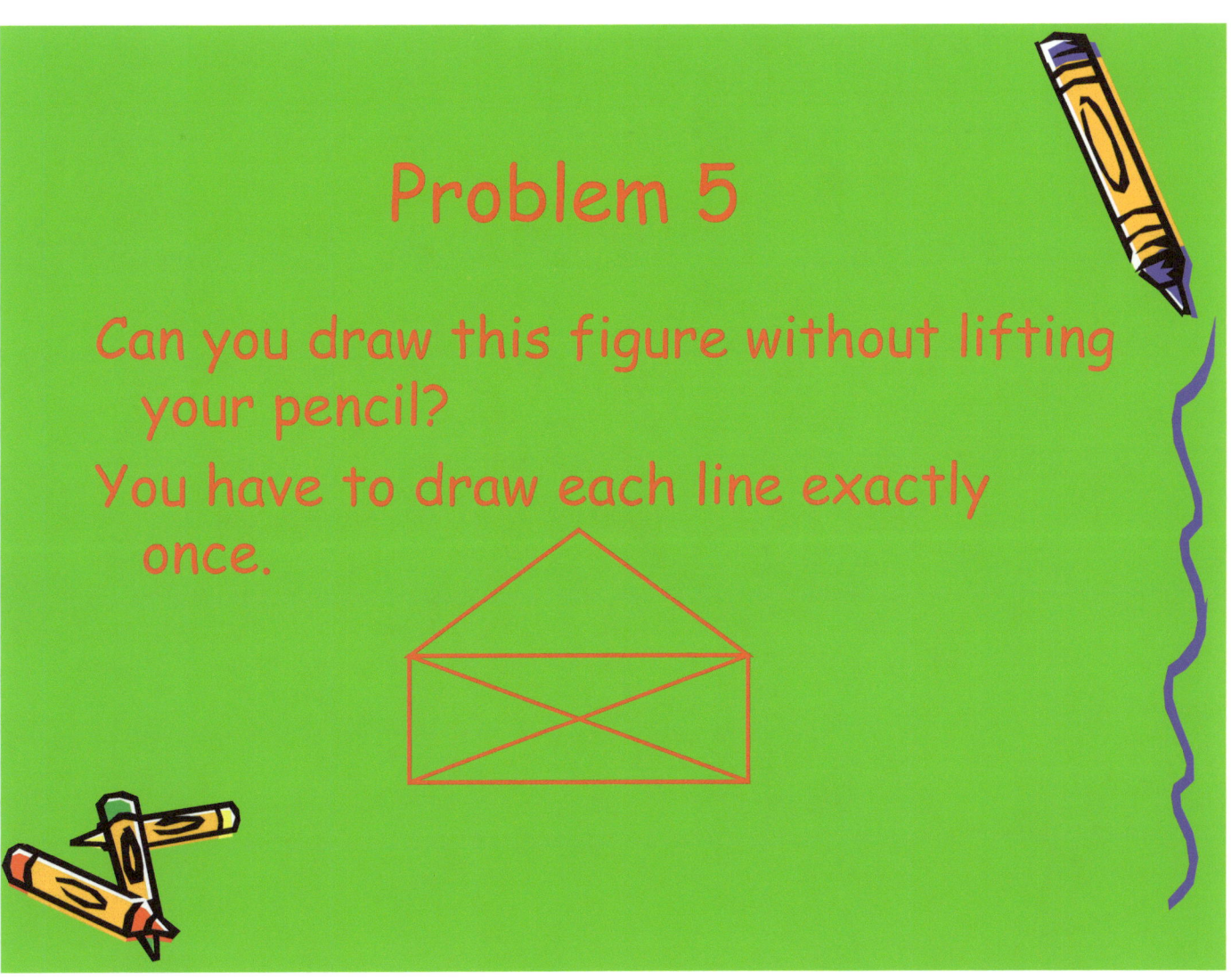

Hint

You can start at point A.

Problem 6

There are nine dots on the picture. Can you draw four segments on it without lifting your pencil, so that those segments pass through all nine dots?

Answer

The four segments are shown on the picture. Start at point A and proceed to points B, C, and D.

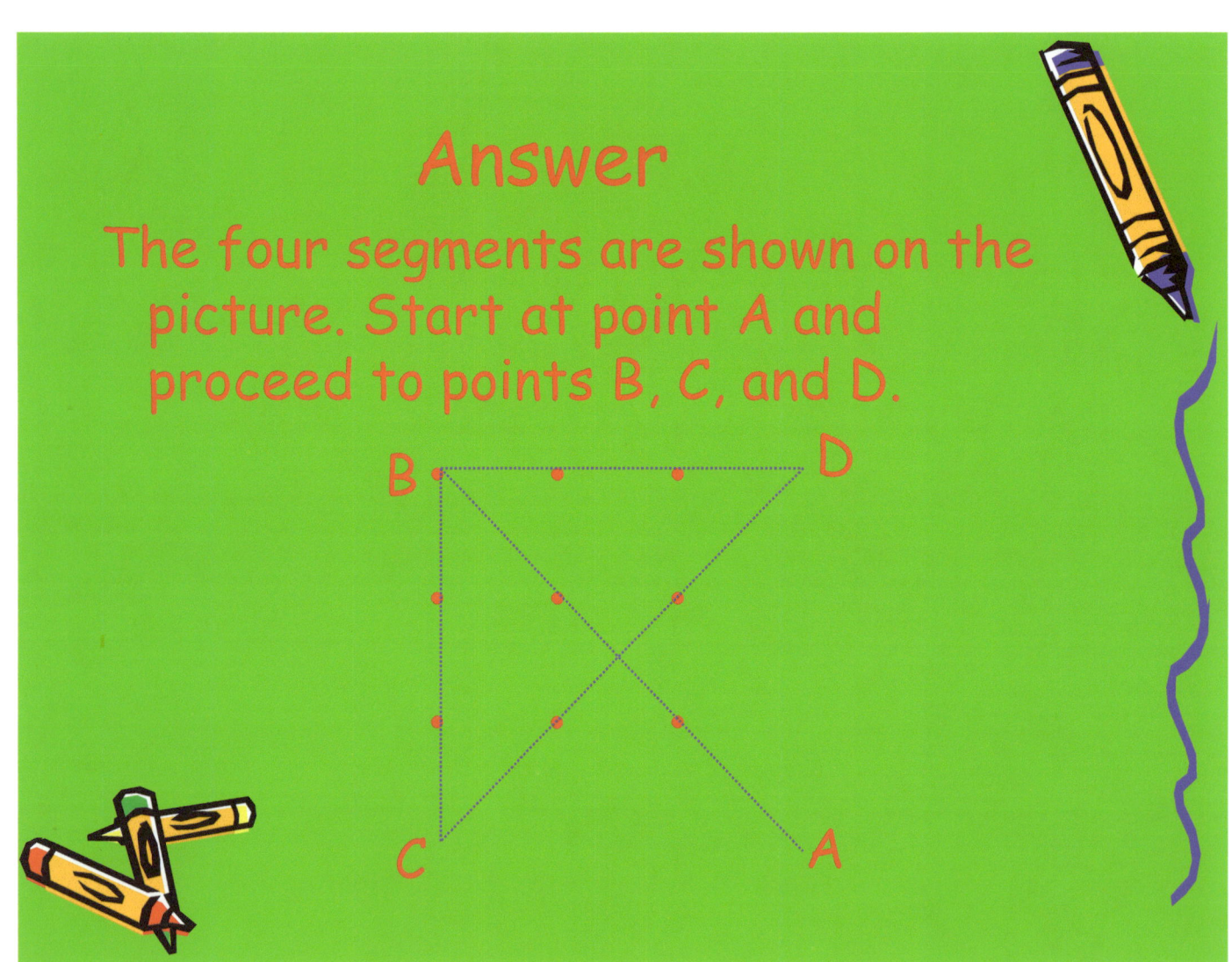

Problem 7

Can you draw this figure without lifting your pencil?

You have to draw each line exactly once.

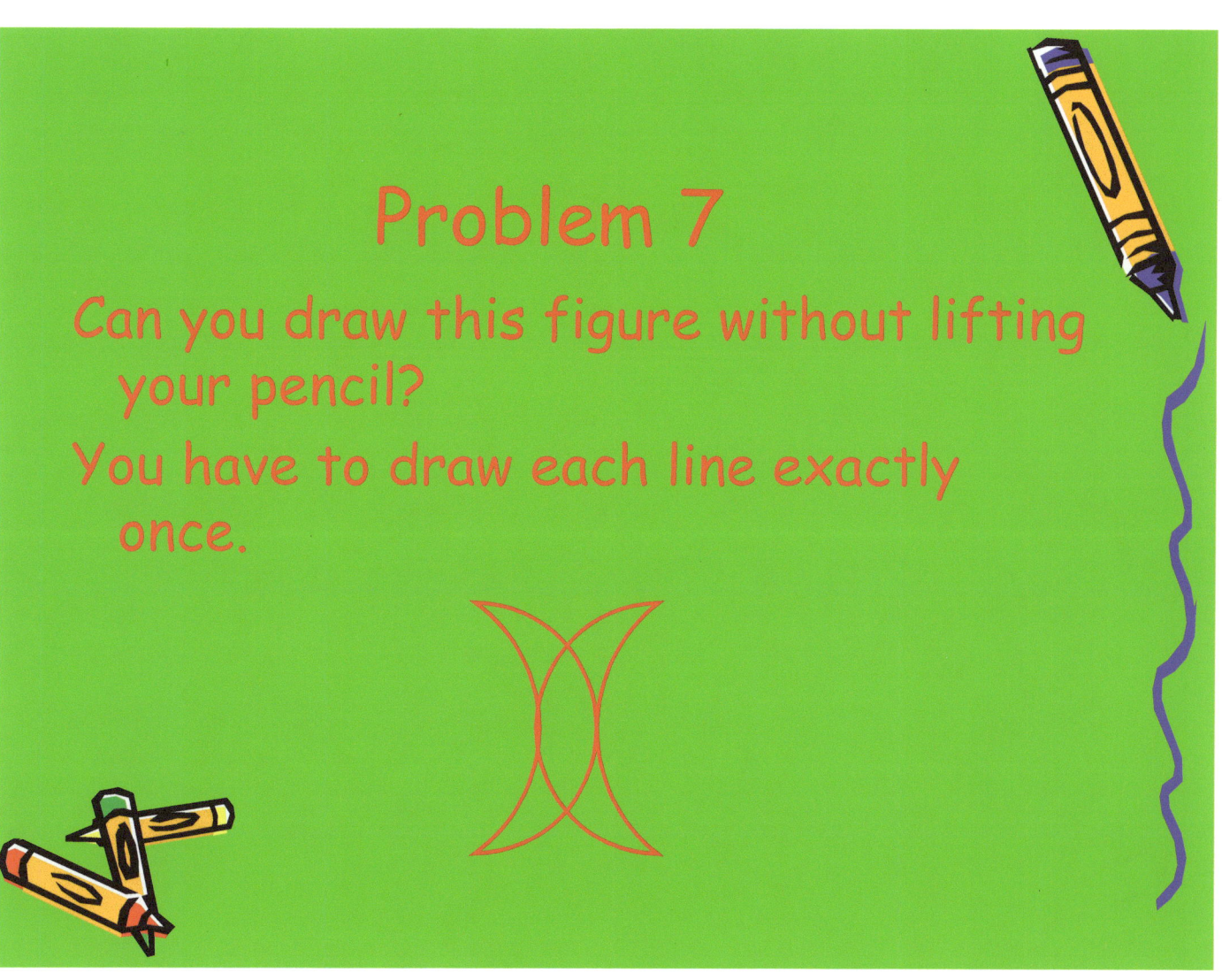

Hint

You can start at point A.

← A

Problem 8

There are four circular bike paths in a park. Can a biker ride through all paths passing each path exactly once?

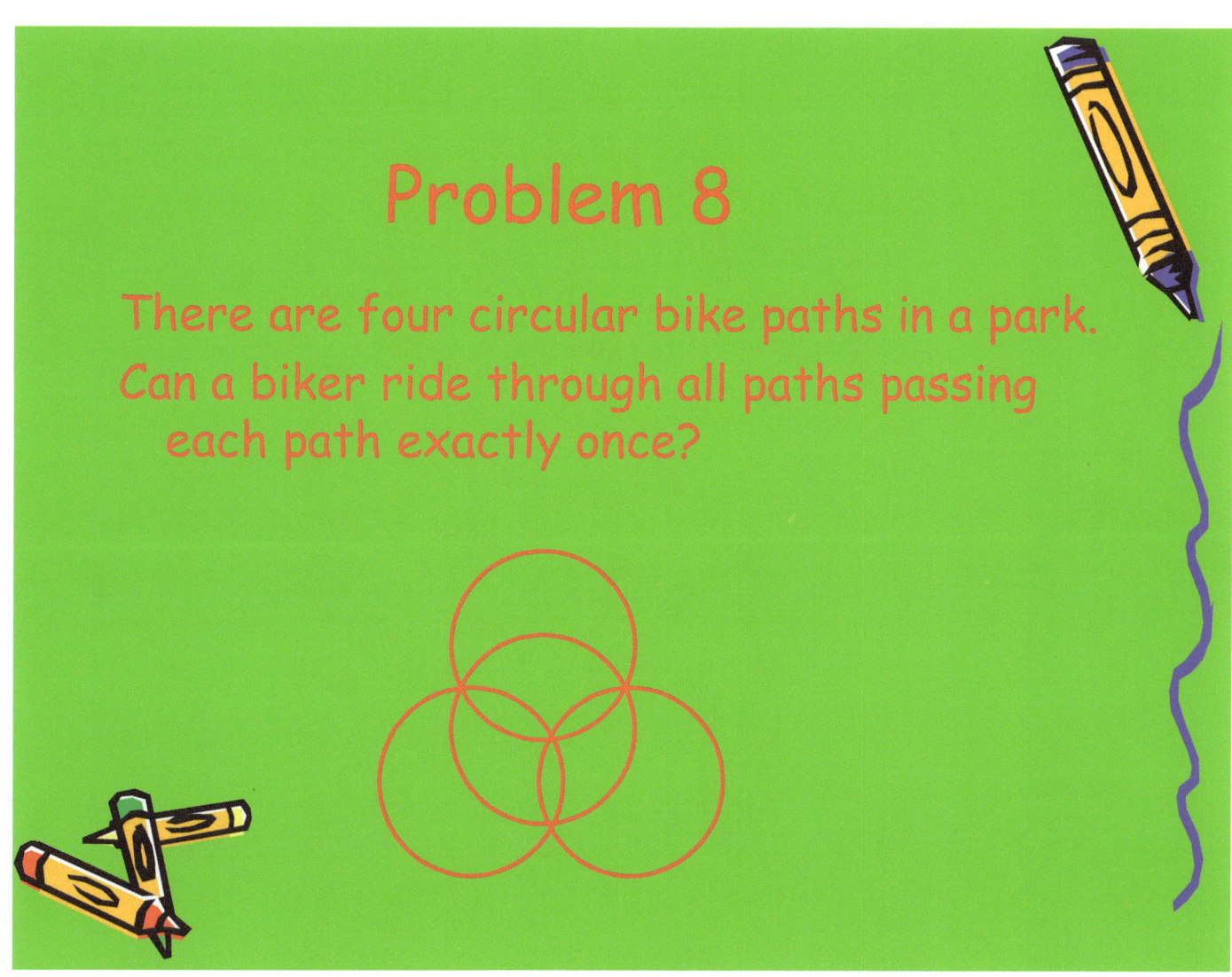

Answer

The biker can start at point A and ride to points B, C, D, E, F, C, H, E, I, A, J, E, H, A, H, C, P, A along red arrows.

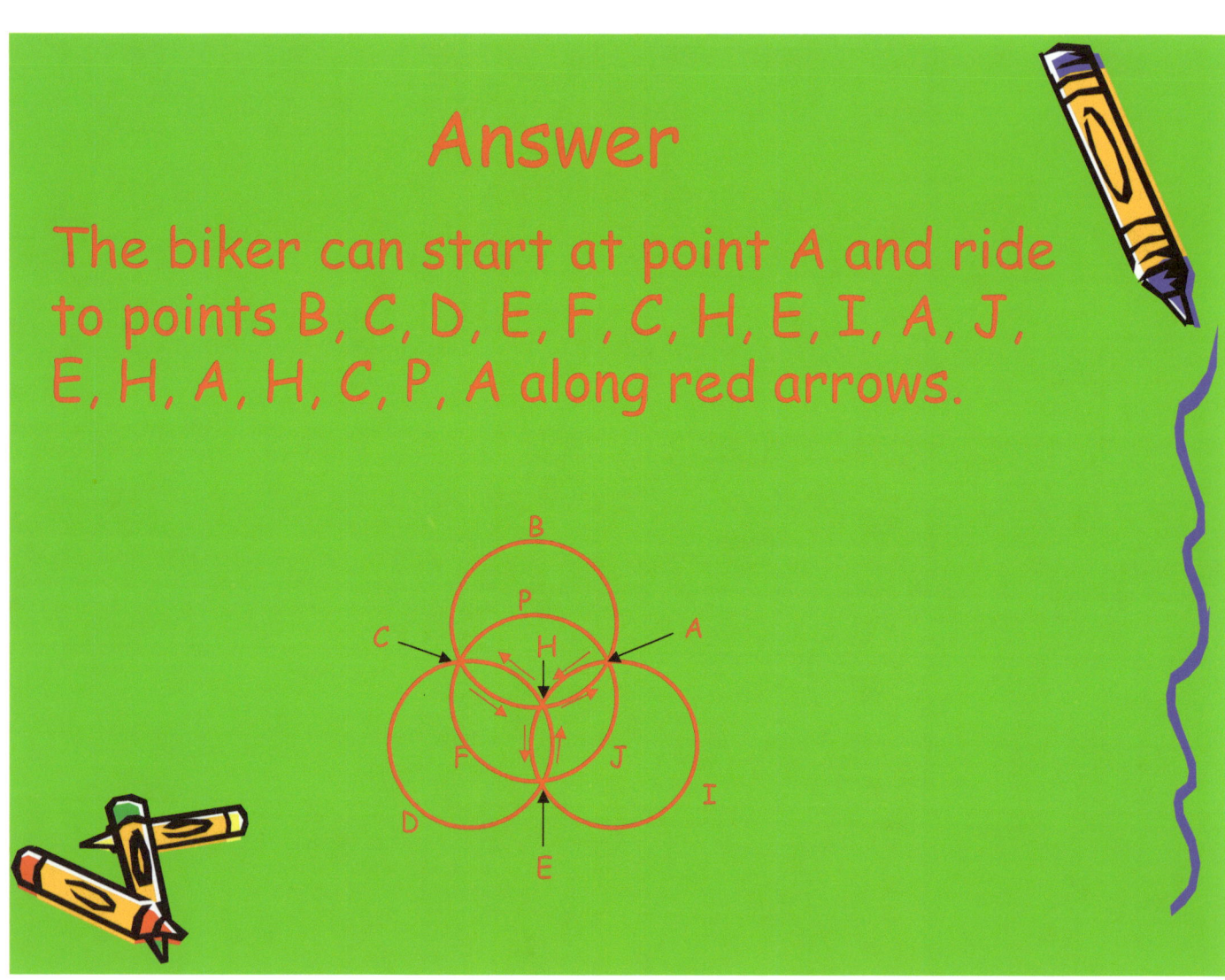

Problem 9

Can you draw this figure without lifting your pencil?

You have to draw each line exactly once.

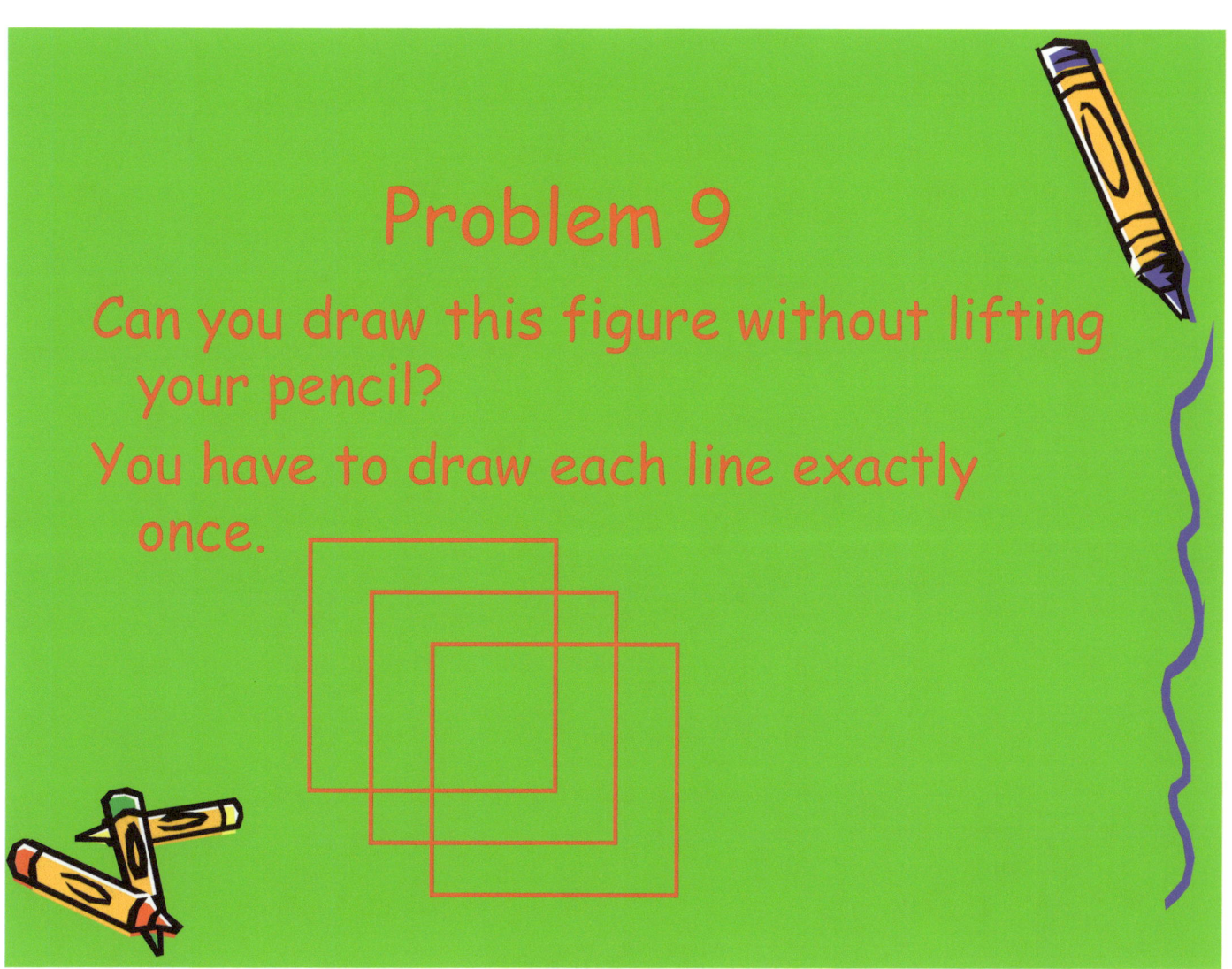

Answer

You can start at point A, draw the left square, move to points B, C, draw the right square, move to points D, E, F, A.

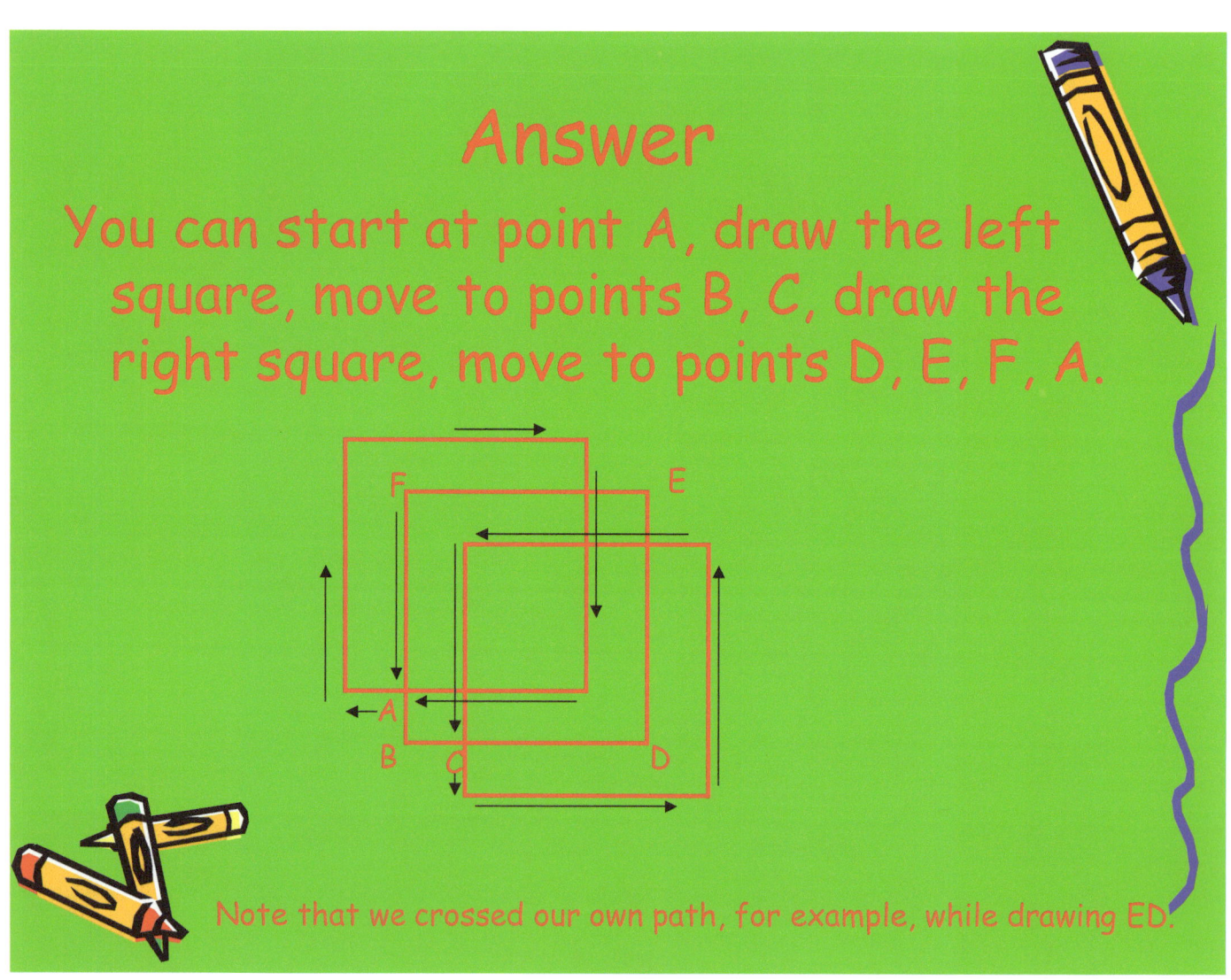

Note that we crossed our own path, for example, while drawing ED.

Problem 10

Can you draw this figure without lifting your pencil?

You have to draw each line exactly once.

You are not allowed to cross your own path.

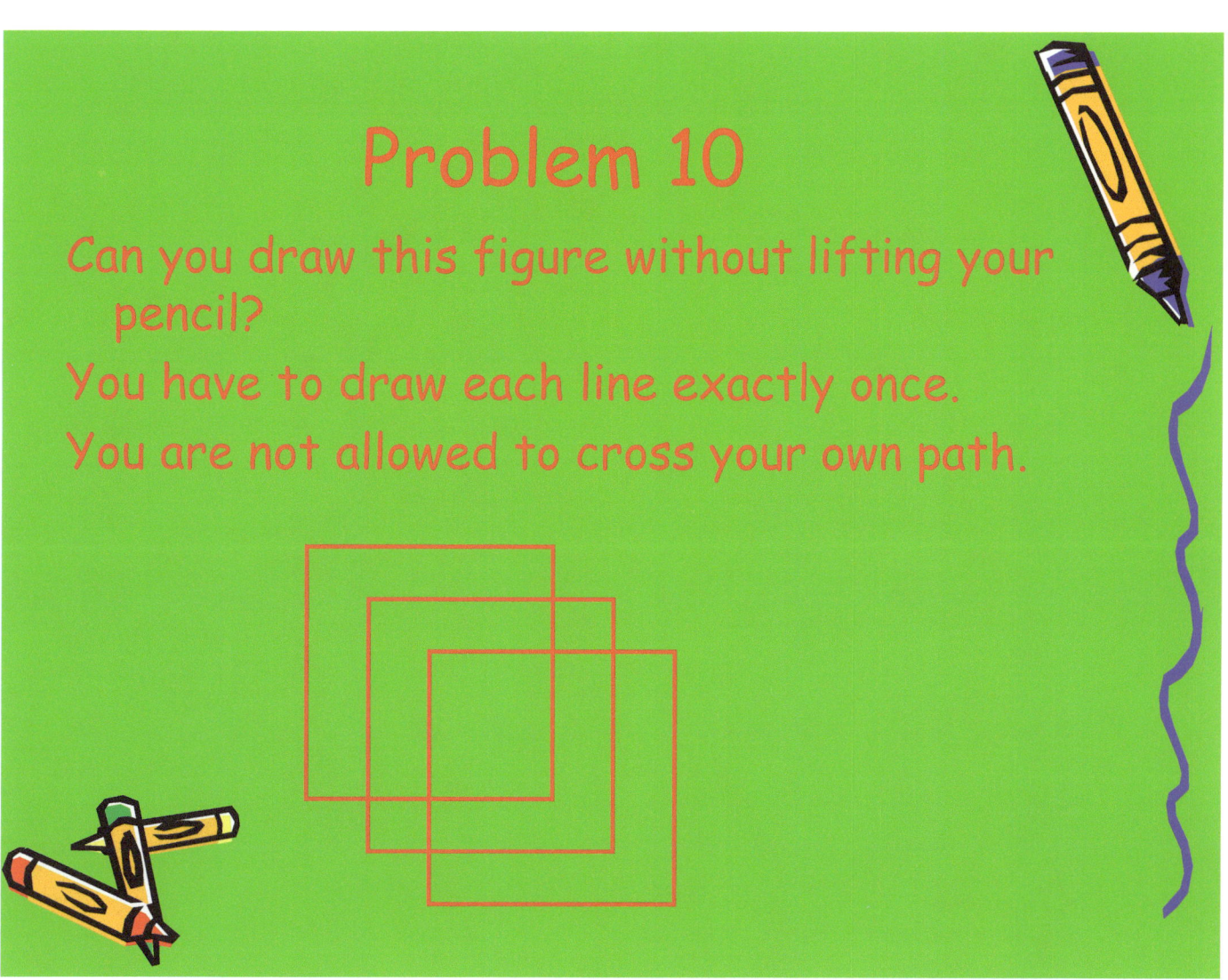

Hint

Paint the figure as shown on the picture.

Answer

Start from point A and follow the boundary of the violet figure.

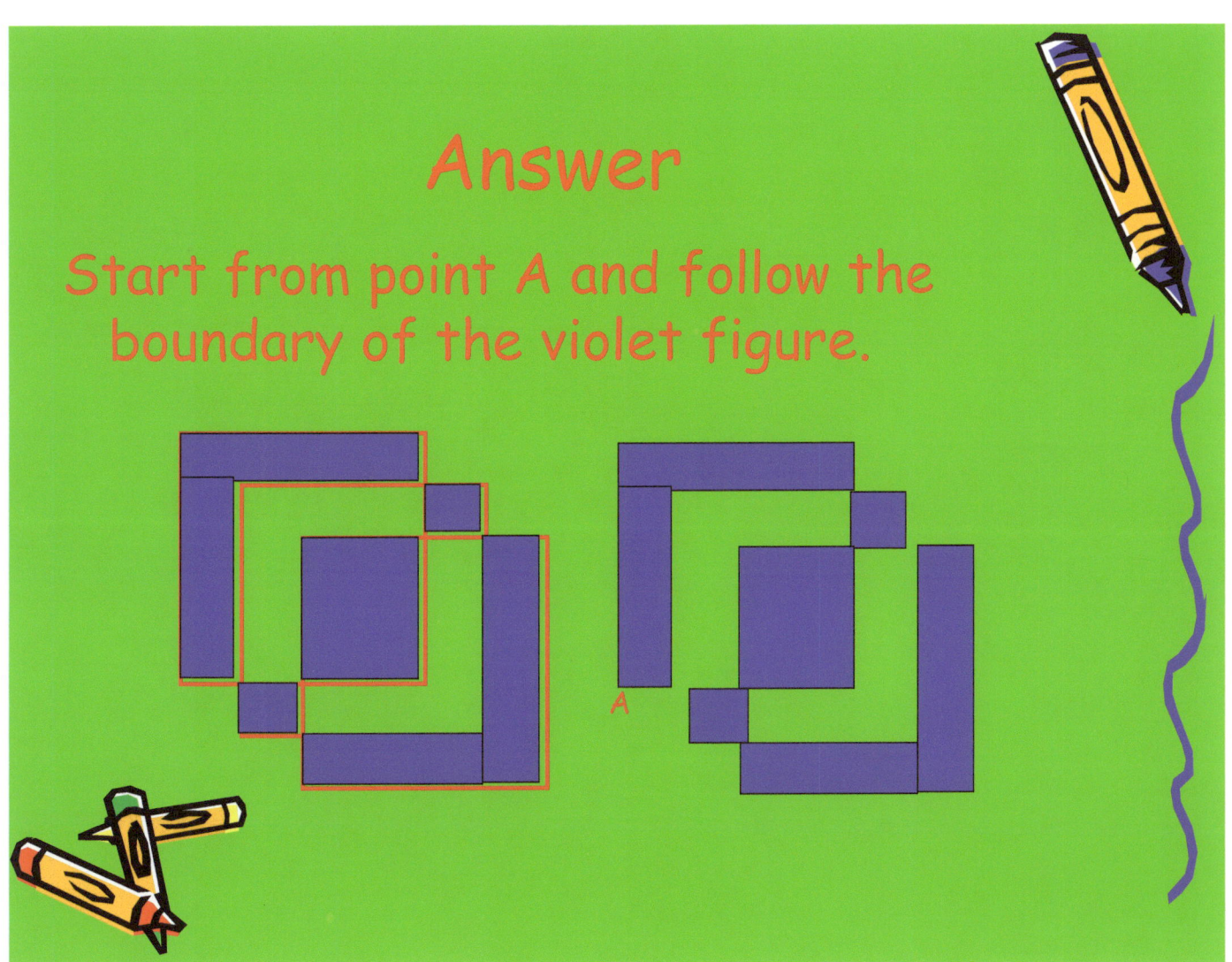

Part 4
Chessboard problems
You don't have to play chess to solve them.

Problem 1

Can one cover an 8 x 8 chessboard with 2 x 1 dominoes?
The dominoes cannot overlap.

Answer

Yes, see the picture below.

and so on.

Problem 2

Can 2 x 2 dominoes cover an 8 x 8 chess board without the upper right square? The dominoes cannot overlap.

Answer

A chess board without the upper right square has 63 squares on it. Each domino piece covers 2 squares. Dominoes can only cover an even number of squares and cannot cover a chess board without one square.

Problem 3

Can you cover an 8 x 8 chessboard without the upper right and lower left square with 2 x 2 dominoes? The dominoes cannot overlap.

Answer

The upper left and lower right squares have the same color, for example, black. The chess board on the picture has 32 white squares and 30 black ones. Each domino piece covers one black and one white square. That means we cannot cover this chessboard with dominoes.

Problem 4

Can one cover an 8 x 8 chessboard without the upper right and upper left square with 2 x 2 dominoes?
The dominoes cannot overlap.

Answer

Yes, see the picture below. Try to continue covering.

Problem 5

Can you cover an 8 x 8 chessboard with 3 x 1 rectangles like the one shown on the picture? They must not overlap.

Pattern

Answer

An 8 x 8 chessboard has 64 squares on it. Each rectangle covers 3 squares. They cannot cover the chessboard, because 64 is not divisible by 3.

Problem 6

Can you cover an 8 x 8 chessboard without the upper right square with the pieces shown on the picture?
The pieces cannot overlap.

  and

Answer

Yes, see the picture below.
Try to continue covering.

Problem 7

Can you cover an 8 x 8 chessboard without the upper right square with pieces like the one shown on the picture? They may not overlap.

Piece

Answer

Yes, see the picture below.
Try to continue covering.

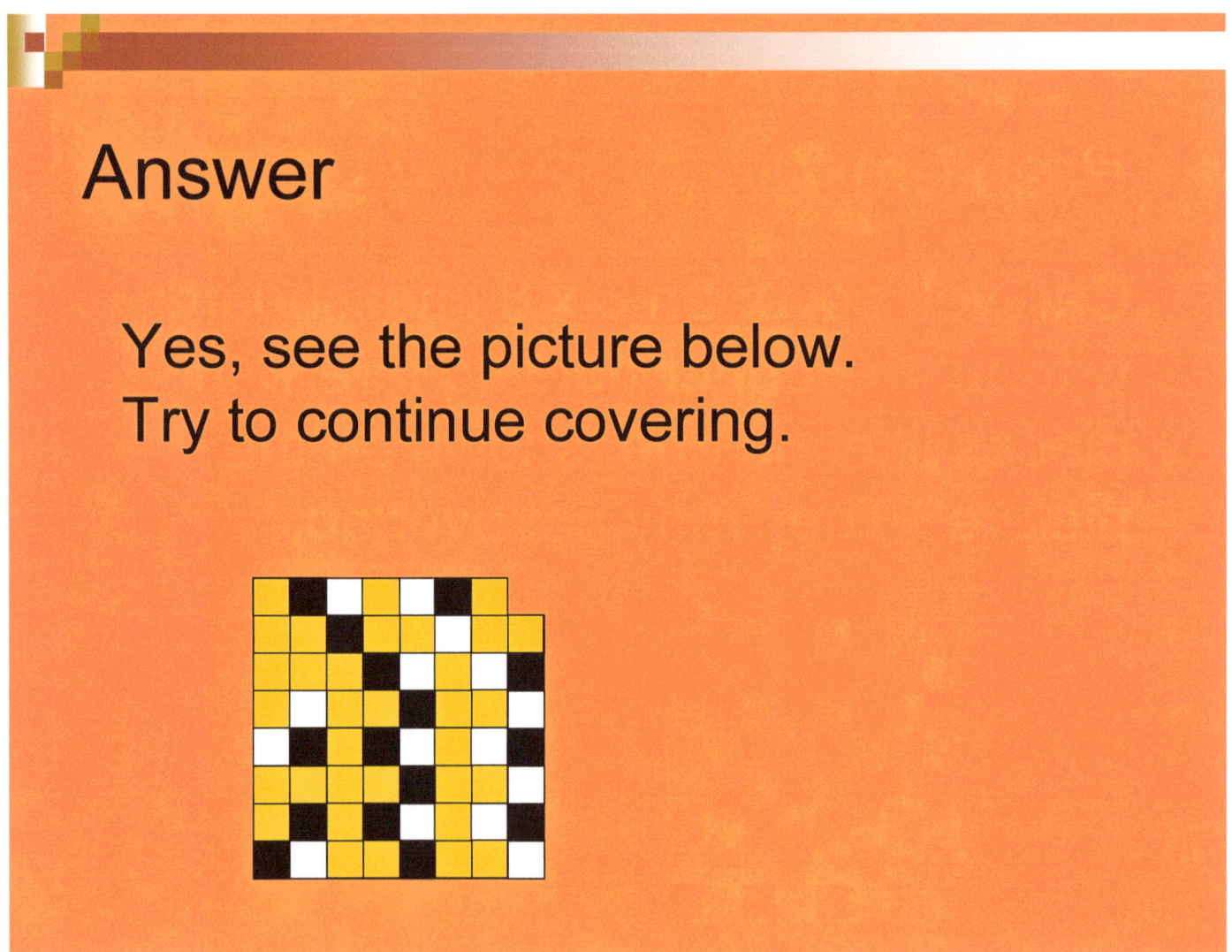

Problem 8

Can you cover an 8 x 8 chessboard without the upper right square with 1 x 3 rectangles like the one shown on the picture? They are not allowed to overlap.

Hint

Paint the chessboard in three different colors.

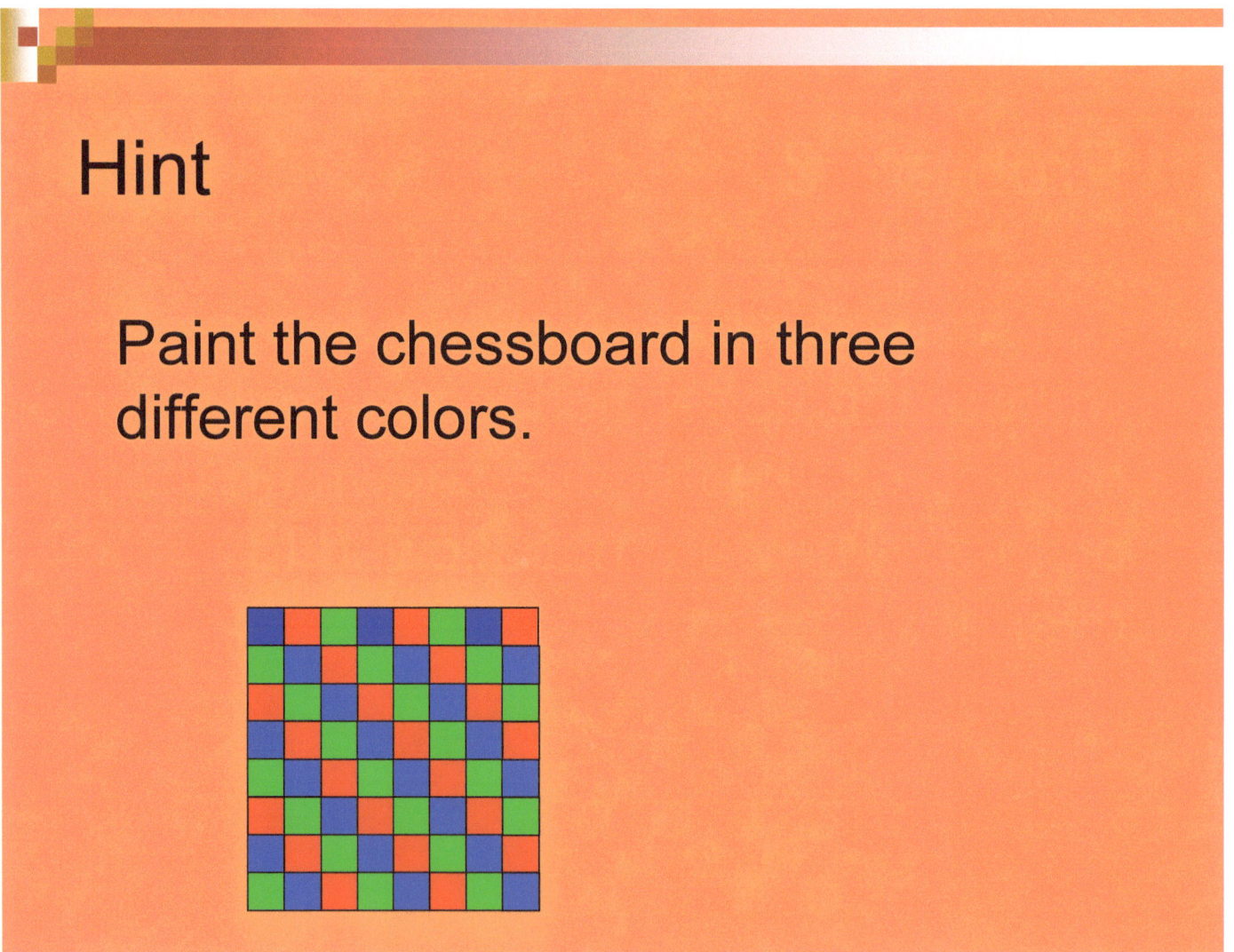

Answer

There are 64 squares on the colored chessboard – 22 blue, 21 red and 21 green. After removing one red corner square, the chess board contains 22 blue, 20 red and 21 green squares. Each 3 x 1 rectangle always covers three different colors. That means that a chessboard without the upper right square cannot be covered by these rectangles.

Problem 9

Can one cover a 10 x 10 chessboard with pieces like the one shown on the picture? The pieces may not overlap.

Hint

Each piece can either cover three white squares and a black one (1), or three black squares and a white one (2).

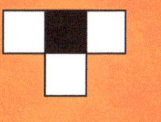 1

 2

Answer

A 10 x 10 chessboard has 100 squares. One piece covers 4 squares. That means we need 25 pieces to cover the board. There is an equal number of black and white squares on the chessboard, therefore we need an equal number of pieces of type 1 and 2. But 25 is not divisible by 2. That means the chessboard cannot be covered by these pieces.

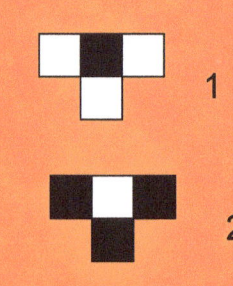

Problem 10

There is a triangle on a chessboard (**a**). One can roll it over any side. Can the triangle occupy the position (**b**) after any number of moves?

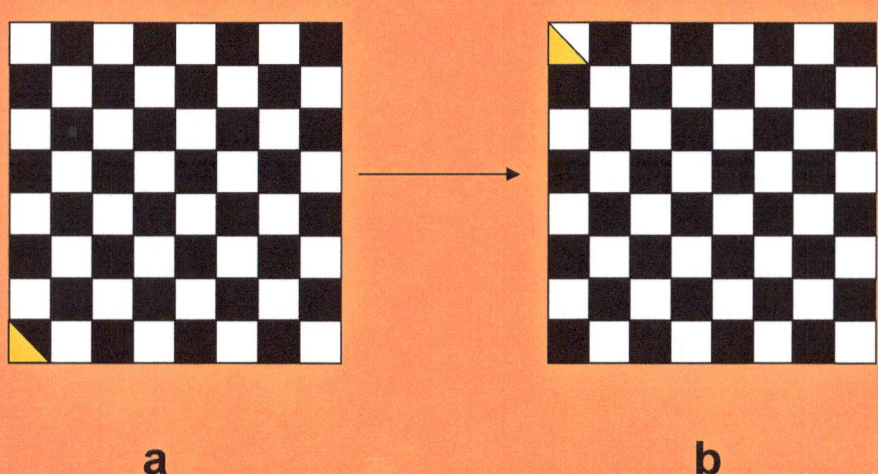

a b

Hint

The long side of the triangle will always go either from the upper left to the lower right corner of a black square, or from the upper right to the lower left corner of a white square.

Answer

The triangle can never occupy position (**b**). When it gets to the top left square, its long side will always go from the upper right to the lower left corner of the square, as shown below.

 or

Part 5

Pouring

We are using the base volume units
1 gallon /gal/ = 4 quarts /qt/
1 quart /qt/ = 2 pints /pt/

Problem 1

Marty has two cans: a small one (5 qt) and a large one (7 qt).
How can he get 6 qt of water from a tap?

Answer

Marty can follow the next steps:
1. Fill the large can with 7 qt of water.
2. Pour 5 qt of water from the large can to the small can.
3. Empty the small can.
4. Pour the remaining 2 qt of water from the large can to the small can.
5. Fill the large can from a tap.
6. Fill the small can from the large can.
7. Empty the small can.
8. Pour the remaining 4 qt of water from the large can to the small can.
9. Fill the large can from a tap.
10. Fill the small can from the large can. Now Marty has 6 qt of water in the large can.

Answer /continued/

These 10 steps are summarized in the following table:

Step	1	2	3	4	5	6	7	8	9	10
Large can	7	2	2	0	7	4	4	0	7	6
Small can	0	5	0	2	2	5	0	4	4	5

Problem 2

There are two buckets – 4 qt and 9 qt. How can you get 6 qt of water from a river?

Answer

You can follow these steps:

Step	1	2	3	4	5	6	7	8
Large can	9	5	5	1	1	0	9	6
Small can	0	4	0	4	0	1	1	4

Problem 3

Kathy has two cans – 3 qt and 5 qt. How can she pour 4 qt of water from a tap?

Answer

Kathy can use the following table:

Step	1	2	3	4	5	6
Large can	5	2	2	0	5	4
Small can	0	3	0	2	2	3

Problem 4

There are three buckets: 10qt, 7qt, and 3qt. The large bucket is full of milk. How can you pour 5 qt of milk into the medium bucket?

Answer

You can follow these steps:

Step	1	2	3	4	5	6	7	8	9
Large bucket	10	3	3	6	6	9	9	2	2
Medium bucket	0	7	4	4	1	1	0	7	5
Small bucket	0	0	3	0	3	0	1	1	3

Problem 5

There are more than 13 gal of gasoline in a container. A driver has two cans – a 9 gal can and a 5 gal can.
How can he get 8 gal of gasoline?

Answer

The driver can use the following table:

Step	1	2	3	4	5	6	7
Container	>13	>4	>4	>9	>9	>0	>0
Large can	0	9	4	4	0	9	8
Small can	0	0	5	0	4	4	5

Problem 6

A large can /12 gal/ is full of milk. A farmer has two empty cans – a small one /5 gal/ and a medium one /8 gal/. How can the farmer divide the milk equally between two cans?

Answer

The farmer can follow these steps:

Step	1	2	3	4	5	6	7	8
Large can	12	4	4	9	9	1	1	6
Medium can	0	8	3	3	0	8	6	6
Small can	0	0	5	0	3	3	5	0

Problem 7

Bill knows that there are more than 10 pt of water in a a can. He has two pots – a small one /5pt/ and a large one /9 pt/. How can he get exactly 6 pt of water?

Answer

Bill can use the following table:

Step	1	2	3	4	5	6	7	8	9	10	11	12	13
Can	>10	>1	>1	>6	>6	>5	>5	>0	>0	>9	>9	>4	>4
Large pot	0	9	4	4	0	0	5	5	9	0	1	1	6
Small pot	0	0	5	0	4	5	0	5	1	1	0	5	0

Problem 8

There are 18 qt of water in a bucket and three empty pots – 7 qt, 7 qt, and 4 qt.

How can you put 6 qt of water in the bucket and 6 qt in each of the two bigger pots?

Answer

You can follow the next steps:

Step	1	2	3	4	5	6	7	8	9	10
Bucket	18	11	11	11	7	7	8	8	8	12
1st pot 7 qt	0	7	3	3	3	3	3	3	6	6
2d pot 7 qt	0	0	0	4	4	7	7	3	0	0
3d pot 4 qt	0	0	4	0	4	1	0	4	4	0

Answer /continued/

Step	11	12	13	14	15	16	17
Bucket	5	5	9	9	2	2	6
1st pot 7 qt	6	6	6	6	6	6	6
2d pot 7 qt	7	3	3	0	7	6	6
3d pot 4 qt	0	4	0	3	3	4	0

Problem 9

Peter has three cans: 6 qt, 7 qt, and 3 qt. He knows that there is 4 qt of water in the first can and 6 qt of water in the second one.

How can he pour half of the water into one can?

Answer

Peter can use the following table:

Step	1	2	3	4	5	6
1st can 6 qt	4	1	1	6	5	5
2d can 7 qt	6	6	7	2	2	5
3d can 3 qt	0	3	2	2	3	0

Problem 10

Grandma put two equal cups – a cup of coffee and a cup of milk - on a table. Then she poured one tablespoon of milk in the cup of coffee and stirred it. After that she poured one tablespoon from the cup of coffee in the cup of milk.
Which is now bigger – the volume of coffee in the cup of milk or the volume of milk in the cup of coffee?

Answer

Let's look at the cup that originally had only coffee. Suppose the volume of that cup is V, and the volume of milk in it is M. The remaining volume in this cup is V-M, and it is coffee. The rest of the coffee that was originally in that cup is now in the other cup. So the amount of coffee in the milk is
V- (V- M) = M
That means Grandma gets the same amounts of coffee in the milk and milk in the coffee.

www.ingramcontent.com/pod-product-compliance
Lightning Source LLC
Chambersburg PA
CBHW041515220426
43668CB00002B/26